HAL HIGDON'S
Half Marathon Training

Hal Higdon

Human Kinetics

Library of Congress Cataloging-in-Publication Data

Names: Higdon, Hal.
Title: Hal Higdon's half marathon training / Hal Higdon.
Description: Champaign, IL : Human Kinetics, [2016] | Includes
  bibliographical references.
Identifiers: LCCN 2015037239 | ISBN 9781492517245 (print)
Subjects: LCSH: Marathon running--Training. | Long distance runners--Training
  of.
Classification: LCC GV1065.17.T73 H54 2016 | DDC 796.42/52--dc23 LC record available at http://lccn.
loc.gov/2015037239

ISBN: 978-1-4925-1724-5 (print)

The web addresses cited in this text were current as of November 2015, unless otherwise noted.

Senior Managing Editor: Elizabeth Evans; **Copyeditor:** Annette Pierce; **Permissions Manager:** Martha
Gullo; **Graphic Designers:** Nancy Rasmus, Denise Lowry, and Fred Starbird; **Cover Designer:** Keith
Blomberg; **Photograph (cover):** iStock.com/lzf; **Photographs (interior):** © Human Kinetics, unless
otherwise noted; **Photo Asset Manager:** Laura Fitch; **Photo Production Manager:** Jason Allen; **Printer:**
United Graphics

Human Kinetics books are available at special discounts for bulk purchase. Special editions or book excerpts
can also be created to specification. For details, contact the Special Sales Manager at Human Kinetics.

Printed in the United States of America   10   9   8   7   6   5   4   3   2   1

The paper in this book is certified under a sustainable forestry program.

Human Kinetics
Website: www.HumanKinetics.com

United States: Human Kinetics, P.O. Box 5076, Champaign, IL 61825-5076
800-747-4457
e-mail: humank@hkusa.com

Canada: Human Kinetics, 475 Devonshire Road Unit 100, Windsor, ON N8Y 2L5
800-465-7301 (in Canada only)
e-mail: info@hkcanada.com

Europe: Human Kinetics, 107 Bradford Road, Stanningley, Leeds LS28 6AT, United Kingdom
+44 (0) 113 255 5665
e-mail: hk@hkeurope.com

Australia: Human Kinetics, 57A Price Avenue, Lower Mitcham, South Australia 5062
08 8372 0999
e-mail: info@hkaustralia.com

New Zealand: Human Kinetics, P.O. Box 80, Mitcham Shopping Centre, South Australia 5062
0800 222 062
e-mail: info@hknewzealand.com

E6660

For the friends who follow me on Facebook.
I learn as much from them as they from me.

Contents

Introduction

Downsizing, clearing out the clutter in our basement, I recently came across a box of plaques: awards accumulated during a long career of running, too many to hang on a wall, so despite all the effort and energy spent winning those plaques, for a long time they had been set aside, stuffed on a shelf, not seen for years. But now what to do with them? Should my wife, Rose, and I force younger family members to accept plaques as fond memories of a grandparent? Should we offer them on eBay to strangers not met, who nevertheless might appreciate them more than we? Or would the plaques be best deposited in a dumpster, to be uncovered centuries later by archeologists curious about an ancient civilization? A civilization that featured running as one of its main recreational activities.

But one plaque at the top of the pile stood out, spoke to me. Made of maple with a golden panel attached, it served as proof that on September 11, 1977, I had won the masters division of the Cleveland Heart-A-Thon.

Heart-a-thon? What exactly was a heart-a-thon? The word fails to attract an entry in the massive *Random House Dictionary of the English Language* that dominates a book shelf in my office. Even the Internet fails to provide a precise definition. Fortunately, the plaque identified the distance of the race I had run—and won—so long, long ago: 13.1 miles!

Thus, a heart-a-thon (at least that one in Cleveland that bygone year) was 13.1 miles, a race distance now more properly identified as a half marathon, half the 26.2 miles of the full marathon that attracts so many to the running sport. And while I do not have a plaque to prove my participation, because I did not run the race, another 13.1-miler emerged that same year (1977) in Indianapolis, its true distance similarly disguised under the label minimarathon. Currently, according to Running USA, the main source of facts and statistics for road racing in the United States, the OneAmerica 500 Festival Mini-Marathon (or Indy Mini) is one of the largest half marathons in the United States with approximately 22,500 finishers in the half in 2015 and another 3,500 finishers in the accompanying 5K. (Gothenburg, Sweden, hosted the world's largest half, with 47,403 finishers that same year.)

As for the *oldest* half marathon, at least in the United States, the Caesar Rodney Half Marathon in Wilmington, Delaware, founded in 1964, might have a claim on that title. Despite its historical claim to fame, Caesar Rodney remains a relatively small event today: 1,245 runners and walkers in a combined 5K and half marathon in 2015.

Heart-A-Thon. Minimarathon. What else? The Philadelphia Distance Run, also founded in 1977, is another 13.1-mile race that still fails to advertise its distance. It was almost as though in the 1970s (the decade when running emerged as a popular participant sport), new runners were embarrassed to admit to running *only* a 13.1-mile race when they could be—maybe should be—running a 26.2-mile race, a full-distance marathon, a more heroic event.

How life changes. No more! Because today certainly no embarrassment exists among people running a half marathon vs. a full marathon. In 2014, according to Running USA, 2,200 half marathons were held in the United States. Nearly four times as many runners participated in half marathons than in full marathons: 2,046,600 vs. 550,637 finishers. On the list of the 100 largest American races, 40 were half marathons. As for trends, the number of half marathon finishers in the United States quadrupled between the years 2000 and 2014.

Why such interest in the half marathon? The obvious reason would seem to be that it is an easier distance for beginning runners to achieve. Less scary. Easier to climb Pikes Peak than Mount Kilimanjaro or Mount Everest. You don't have to train as many weeks or miles. Training for a half marathon thus fits more conveniently into a busy lifestyle than training for a full marathon. My half marathon training programs (provided later in this book) last 12 weeks compared to 18 weeks for full marathons. The weekly mileage for my half programs is somewhat less. The daily mileage also is somewhat less. For example, the maximum long run for runners using my novice 1 half marathon training program is 10 miles (16 km) instead of 20 miles (32 km) for full marathons. An easier path to glory would seem to be one reason for the half's popularity, except I'm not sure that remains entirely true, or at least it is not the only reason.

In many respects, a half marathon presents a tougher challenge than the full distance—at least for beginners. Not to discourage anybody, but it may be more difficult to go from 0 miles to 13.1 miles than it is to go from 13.1 miles to 26.2 miles. By the time you have trained for and run a half marathon, that's quite a feat in my mind. You have achieved a high level of physical fitness; you have mentally conditioned yourself to become a Runner (in caps). Move up to a full marathon? Piece of cake. You're a runner now. Train a half dozen more weeks. Add a few more weekly miles. You're there.

But back to the half marathon's historical roots: As recently as a decade ago, the half marathon did not possess the *gravitas* that it possesses today. Beginning runners looked past Pikes Peak and Kilimanjaro and focused first on Everest. For many, the marathon was their first long-distance running race, a fact that often both puzzled and confounded grizzled veterans. Runners who had been in the sport more than a couple of years often suggested to newbies: "Uh, wouldn't you like to try a 5K or a 10K first, just to get a feel for the sport?" No, they wanted the marathon, the full monty. Thirteen? In days of old, that number existed only as a mile marker en route to twenty-six.

That has changed. Today's runners, new and old, think differently. Perhaps it is because of the marketing skills of people organizing half marathons. (Competitor Group, based in San Diego, California, sponsors more than 30 half marathons around the world as part of its Rock 'n' Roll series.) Perhaps it is because of the emergence of female competitors as a dominant force in running. I find the following statistic delicious. Sixty-one percent of half marathon finishers in 2014 were women. Yes, ladies, you are more than here.

Excuse me for throwing in a bit of historical perspective: I'm old enough to remember when women actually were *barred* from running marathons. Barred and *banned*, threatened with loss of official sanction from what was then the U.S. governing body, the Amateur Athletic Union. Run more than a few miles in a race and you could lose your so-called amateur status, the same as if you had accepted prize money or used performance-enhancing drugs. It wasn't until 1966 that Roberta Gibb Bingay broke the sex barrier at the Boston Marathon, and several men initially thought she had not run the full distance, because women supposedly were incapable of such a feat. (Bobbi did run the distance, and she and tens of thousands of female runners who followed have proved over the years that they are more than equal to men.)

But let's give deserved credit to male runners, too, when it comes to the half marathon's current status. Perhaps the uptick in the popularity of the half is because experienced runners (men and women), who might run one or two marathons a year, fill in the time between those 26-mile journeys with 13-mile mini-journeys, which do not take quite as much preparation or loss of family time. Perhaps it is because in my 18-week marathon training programs, I now suggest that runners run a half marathon in week 8 or 9 as a test race. For whatever reason, the half marathon now rules running, at least in numbers.

And for all of those reasons I now present you with *Hal Higdon's Half Marathon Training*. Are you a beginner? I'll show you how to start and offer all the information you, a nouveau runner, needs to know. Shoes, strength training, stretching? It's all here in the book you now hold in your hands. Are you an experienced runner? I'll show you how to continue in your favorite sport, how to run more comfortably, if not faster. (Well, faster, too.) Are you a dedicated out-of-my-way-because-I'm-fast runner? Although the focus often seems to have shifted to the midpack, there's plenty of room in this sport for you, too. Here is what else I have to offer in *Hal Higdon's Half Marathon Training*: Programs! Programs! Programs!

The heart of this book is programs for runners of all speeds. Novice. Intermediate. Advanced. Programs if you want to run three days a week, four days a week, five days a week, six days a week, although not seven days a week because I strongly believe most runners deserve at least one day of rest. Regardless of your level, pick your program. And if these programs are not enough, I'll even teach you in a final chapter how to design a do-it-yourself half marathon program.

Welcome to my world. Welcome to the running life that began for me when I first went out for track as a sophomore in high school, a life that has continued until this day. Welcome to fitness. Welcome to good health. Welcome to *Hal Higdon's Half Marathon Training*. You are about to become a better runner at today's most popular racing distance.

—Hal Higdon
Long Beach, Indiana

1 | An Incredible Journey

A magic moment occurs when we step out the door and take our first tottering steps as runners. For those readers of this book—old runners, wise runners, experienced runners—who have been running more than a few weeks, more than a few months, more than a few years, you remember that moment, don't you? Humor me while I speak to the newcomers of our sport. For those of you who only have begun to contemplate those first steps, you are about to embark on an incredible journey. That journey, those steps, will take you through a widening portal revealing a path aimed at the finish line of a 13-mile, 192.5-yard race. A half marathon! This is a journey that will change your life. *Consider:* You will be able to attach a 13.1-mile sticker to the back of your car with honor.

But how do you begin that journey? How do you proceed without embarrassment? How do you continue without hurting too much? Runners sometimes suffer injuries, or at least sore muscles. You've heard all about that, haven't you, from well-meaning friends who might laugh when you admit that you want to become a runner. "A runner? You can't be serious? Your knees: You'll ruin your knees!" Ignore those people. Don't challenge them with the proven fact that sedentary people suffer more knee problems than those of us who exercise. Proceed anyway with the guarantee from me right now that eventually friends and family and strangers will learn to respect your commitment to a new life.

But for the time being, you *do* have worries. You *do* have questions. Every new runner has questions. And old (experienced) runners still have questions, too. I plan to answer them all so that by the time you turn the final page, you will be a knowledgeable runner. Here are a few questions that you probably have as you begin to read this book. Here also are my brief answers.

1. **Shoes?** Start by buying a good pair that are properly fitted. Go to a running specialty shop, not to a discount store in an outlet mall.

2. **Strength training?** I favor pumping iron for fitness if not for fast times. But if you are not already a gym rat, wait until after you finish your first half marathon to start strength training.

3. **Stretching?** Warm your muscles first before you attempt to stretch them. That may mean stopping after the first mile or waiting until you finish.

4. **Cross-training?** When I prescribe *cross* in my training programs, I mean an aerobic exercise such as biking or swimming or even walking. Beware of superfit routines that might cause injury.

5. **Speed work?** Essential if you want to improve performance, but maybe not wise for newbies and oldies also need to speed train with caution.

6. **Nutrition?** Here's the golden rule: 55 percent carbohydrate, 30 percent fat, 15 percent protein. Forget fad diets. Go high carbohydrate for endurance.

7. **Weight loss?** Can you lose weight while training for a half marathon? Maybe, but cutting too many calories can impair performance, both during training and on race day.

8. **Gear and gadgets?** OMG, you can go broke in a hurry buying GPS watches and the like. Great for motivation, but running remains a low-cost sport.

9. **Racing?** Scared of the masses? Don't get anxious. Road racing is not an exclusive sport. I will ease your entry into it.

10. **Programs?** Which training program should you follow? *Whoa!* The entire second half of this book is crammed with programs. Please be patient.

Yes, those are some obvious questions, but although my answers are brief, I will address all of your questions as you continue to read *Hal Higdon's Half Marathon Training.*

Let's get serious. Precisely, what do you need to know on that day when you stick your head out the door of your house or apartment and (gulp) look both ways up and down the street, hoping that nobody is looking? Yes, taking those first few steps is not easy. Who said it was easy? If other runners told you starting to run was easy, they were wrong. It is not. Or maybe they just have forgotten. You put your first foot forward, then you put your other foot forward. That's all it takes. *Yeah, right!*

Once you're running, next thing you know, you'll be competing in your first half marathon.
Marathonfoto.com

Running is not necessarily easy. Mea culpa: It takes a certain amount of courage for one thing. One woman contacting me on Facebook admitted that she was *petrified* at the thought of running a half marathon. But don't worry. I said to her as I say to you: Help is on the way. In fact, help already is in your hands within the pages of this book, not only my words, my support, my knowledge, but also the words, support, and knowledge of all my friends, both new runners and old runners and a lot of runners in between.

Courage Is the Key

Contemplating the writing of *Hal Higdon's Half Marathon Training*, I enlisted social media, those friends who follow me on Facebook. I asked several questions, starting with the most obvious, "How did you begin?"

> *For those of you who have been running more than a few months, do you remember those first few stumbling steps out the door, your first workout, your first run? What questions did you have? Have they been answered now? Thinking back on that first run, what do you know now that you wish you had known then?*

The responses proved fascinating. Elizabeth Dawn Taylor, a waitress and writer from Canton, New York, began to run at age 47, after back surgery. "I could run only about 50 yards," Taylor recalls. "It took me two years to get to the half marathon, running at an 8:32 pace per mile (5:18/km). I'm happier and healthier than ever. When I was younger, I liked to run a few miles here and there, but never as much as I do now."

Julie Roth, 29, a professor at Odessa College in St. Charles, Illinois, did not remember her first run, but she remembered starting running in seventh grade around the time her parents divorced. Roth says, "I didn't realize it then, but running became a way for me to escape the trauma of my life and learn to take care of myself."

Although my half marathon training programs have been readily available and free on the Internet since back in the 1990s, Nancy Caviness, 56, owner of a bed and breakfast in Duck, North Carolina, did not immediately find them. Caviness reports, "I cobbled together a way to get ready for my first 10-mile (16.1 km) race. Did some things wrong, some things right. Guidance for me as a beginner would have been very welcome."

Guidance today is much more available both for beginners and seasoned runners. A reservoir of knowledge exists, at least partly because of the popularity of the half marathon, because of the increasing number of people, young and old who choose 13.1094 miles (or 21.0475 km) as their first race distance, their first love. Here is my guarantee to you: You are not alone.

Is there a single best formula for success? "No one has all the answers for how best to train," writes Jack Daniels, PhD, in *Daniels' Running Formula*, "and there is no single system that works best for everybody" (2014, p. ix). True, but some systems work better than others, and I'm going to offer my take on the subject of half marathon training. What are some of the other questions that runners ask, or wish they had asked, when they first began to run?

Running Questions and Answers

Looking back, Sara Huckeba Peek, 39, an administrative aid from Halfmoon, New York, wished that someone had told her about the importance of having the right running shoes vs. the discount pair she first bought at the mall. "Proper fit. Proper feel. I could have avoided a lot of beginner problems with shin splints and sore feet if someone had taken me by the hand and escorted me to a running specialty shop."

Vickie Rhiddlehoover Boggio, 45, an investment advisor from Longview, Texas, did the Couch-to-5K program the summer before her 40th birthday. That's a training program designed by another coach, and there are a lot of programs available on the Internet, free and not free, for beginning runners. Most of them are good, because the most important move a new runner can make is just what that program suggests: Get off the couch! Get out and run! Boggio recalls her first, nonstop, 20-minute run and how amazed she felt that she actually did it. "I also remember," Boggio says, "how hard it was every single time I went out the door."

Boggio made a rookie mistake. Living in Texas, she started running in the summer after work when heat and humidity were at their peak. "I wish somebody had told me to go running before work when it was at least somewhat cooler." Small change in lifestyle for maximum comfort, but Boggio survived her rookie mistake and became a seasoned veteran. And so will you! Boggio adds, "Also, I wish I'd learned earlier that cotton socks are a big no-no!"

Marie Travis, 27, a graphic artist from Lindenhurst, New York, admits she started cluelessly, using a 5K program on her iPod, not even sure whether there were races of that distance in her area. Travis also wondered, "Am I wearing the right shoes? Is this a good pace?" Through trial and error, running eventually became easier for her.

It also took Courtney Jewel Hagermann, 28, an attorney from Bel Air, Maryland, time to learn that everyone has bad runs. Not every run offers a perfect experience. The legendary runner's high? Well, some days you hit it and some days not. The weather may be too hot or too cold or too windy. You may have had a disagreement with your spouse, and the kids were total brats at breakfast, and let's not even talk about your boss at work. *Ugh!* How do you say *jerk* in 47 languages? You may run too fast at the beginning of your workout—and too slow at the end of it. A race for which you had trained for 12 weeks turns into a disappointing experience. "You will have good days and bad days," instructs Hagermann. "This was one of the hardest lessons I learned, but one that has kept me running. The good days far outnumber the bad days."

Angela Redden, 40, a stay-at-home mom, from Stafford, Virginia, started running on a treadmill. "When I got off the treadmill, I cried because it was hard for me, and I felt so heavy. My knees hurt. My shins hurt. I had good shoes, but my body was adjusting to this new form of torture. I wish I had known at the time that that was normal. I also wish I had known how *very* different running outside was compared to running indoors on a treadmill. At first I hated running outside, because of the hills. But soon running hills was what I liked best, because of the extra challenge they offered, the sense of accomplishment you felt after finishing. Now I still get sore and stiff after certain workouts, but I recognize that this is part of the game. This is part of the price you pay for being a runner. Take a day off, and you'll be back to feeling normal, in fact, better than normal. Now I love running outdoors. I would rather run in the pouring rain or the freezing cold than to get back on that treadmill."

Janet Alesna, 47, a physical therapist from Omaha, Nebraska, thought she could never run. "I tried for years," she recalls. "I worked out a lot, but rarely went for a run. I spent so much money on Pilates, reformer training, personal training. You name it; I've done it. Everything except running. I would run a half mile, then pay for it for weeks. 'How can this be fun,' I thought. 'Why would anybody want to be a runner? Where's the enjoyment?'"

Alesna, nevertheless, would not give up: "I had a friend who ran marathons, so I e-mailed him and asked for some tips. My goal was just to run a mile without pain. With my friend providing motivation, I got through that. The next challenge was to go a little further. Then a little further beyond that further. Then my friend convinced me to train for a marathon and do my debut in Chicago, because it's fun. *What?* I told him he must be out of his mind. *Fun?* You cannot be serious! Until then, I had never done a race, never a 5K, never a half marathon. 'Running a race is not hard,' my friend told me. 'You just train for it.' *Yeah, right.* But he was right, and gradually I upped my mileage from 2 to 3 miles (3.2-4.8 km), then to 4 to 5 miles (6.4-8 km), then up into the double digits, but because I was gradually increasing my distance and also, at my friend's advice, not pushing the pace, something clicked. Running did not get easier, but it also did not get that much harder." Alesna finished her first road race at age 45 and continues this day to participate in half marathons and races at other distances.

An Important Secret

With the help of her friend, Janet Alesna had stumbled onto the secret of effective training. Listen up, everybody, because this is important. Very important! *You train up to the point of pain, but you do not run past that point!*

You start slow. You start easy. You run at what I call a conversational pace, a pace easy enough that you can maintain a conversation with a running partner. You start to run distances that you can handle, even if that distance is only to the end of your block. If a certain distance seems too far, if the pace seems too fast, edging you over the pain barrier, you back off and do your next workout at a somewhat shorter distance. And at a slower pace, maybe programming in some walking breaks.

Yes, you can walk in the middle of a run and still consider yourself a runner. Don't listen to so-called experts who try to throw ridiculous rules your way, who say you have to run every step of every race and workout. After a few days of rest and recovery, you resume your journey and run a bit farther. And by going at it slowly, you may suddenly realize that you have pushed the point of pain somewhat further up the road. Eventually you will find yourself standing on the starting line of a half marathon—and soon after that, crossing the finish line of that 13.1-mile race.

Stacey Saunders, 38, a stay-at-home mom from Irmo, South Carolina, ticks off the lessons she learned on the way to becoming a half-marathoner: "Investing in a great pair of running shoes fitted by a trained person, moisture-wicking socks, and Body Glide were some of my first 'lessons learned the hard way.' Since then, through trial and error and reading, I've learned about pacing, proper nutrition, and what technology is best for me." Saunders underlines her most important lesson: "Running does not need to be complex and technical."

Secrets of Success

Do you want to achieve success as a runner? It may be easier than you think. Here are some tips to help you to the finish line of your next half marathon.

Be consistent. If following a training program, actually follow it. Yes, you can miss a run here or a strength session there and still reach your goal, but consistent training is essential for success. If necessary, rearrange your calendar to maintain consistency.

Commit yourself. Get a good plan and stick to it. Pick your goal and dedicate yourself to reaching it. Training now and then when it is convenient will not help you reach that goal.

Train faster. Push yourself and get out of your comfort zone, even if only for a few hundred meters at the end of an easy run. Rest and stress do fit together.

Train farther. The most successful training programs feature gradual but steady increases in distance. A 3-mile run becomes a 4-mile run. A 5-mile run becomes a 6-mile run. Eventually you will find yourself at a starting line ready to run 13.1 miles.

Hire a coach. Think you can do it alone? You probably can, but having a coach (even an online coach) telling you what to do and (more important) what not to do will make running so much easier.

Seek speed. If you run easy all the time, you may continue to improve, but you will improve more if you learn to embrace speed-work. Weekend-long runs are great, but will only get you so far.

Widen out. No single approach will ensure you reach your goal. Consider various options. Success usually is based on combining endurance, speed, recovery, rest, diet, and race strategy. When they all come together, success will be the inevitable reward.

Plan ahead. Go into your half marathon with a plan, hopefully one of mine. What works best usually is an easy start and a hard finish. Stay on schedule for that plan all through the race.

Slow down. Every workout need not feature a flat-out sprint. Particularly in the long runs, slow down to a very comfortable pace. This will allow you to feel more refreshed during your midweek workouts.

Partner up. Seek support from other runners. Sometimes running with a group can add extra fun to your training routine. Club runs will allow you to meet others. Also consider joining a pace team during your half marathon.

Don't despair. Define your own level of success. Own your accomplishment, even if you miss your planned PR.

Did I say that running was supposed to be painful?
Ryan Bethke

Kristan Alvarez, 32, who works at a portrait studio in San Antonio, Texas, remembers her first run: "I was tired after a quarter mile (400 m), since it was only six weeks after having my fourth child. I asked myself, 'Why am I trying to run 13.1?'" She smiles as she states, "The answer is totally obvious to me now."

Listen closely to me, beginners: You are not alone! Said that before, and I'll say that again. Don't let minor aches and pains discourage you from embracing running as a sport. It will get easier. I guarantee that fact to be true.

James McGuire was among the many runners who struggled as a beginner. "As a way to stay healthy and challenge myself, I decided to go 'running' along a creek trail near my house," he says. "What a disaster. I had no idea at all what I was doing. This led to multiple injuries (especially with my knees), to the point where I could hardly walk downstairs, much less run."

After a long period of rest and some soul searching, McGuire decided to give running one more chance, deciding to become better informed on the subject. "I drove to the local bookstore and bought a couple of running-themed books. I learned how running works, how it actually affects your body, the effective ways to train up to longer distances. Am I ever glad I did that. I've since completed seven half marathons and two full marathons and countless 5 and 10Ks."

Now you can use *Hal Higdon's Half Marathon Training* to prepare for this increasingly popular distance. Running is a simple sport. We all learned to run as children, although many of us have forgotten how easy running can be. Through this book, you will come to know the half marathon and also learn how to master it.

The message is clear, everybody. Running is not easy, but accept that as a challenge. John Bingham, famous as a motivational author and speaker and *Runner's World* columnist, states "The miracle isn't that I finished. The miracle is that I had the courage to start." Be part of that miracle now: Start! Get going. I'll see you at the finish line.

2 | Roots

The Indiana Convention Center, located in downtown Indianapolis, across the street from the Indiana State Capitol, is a massive building larger than an aircraft carrier, 1,300,000 square feet (120,774 m^2), its main corridor half a mile (800 m) long, four city blocks along West Maryland Street from Capitol Avenue to West Street. On a Friday afternoon in early May, I encountered a corridor filled with eager runners, coming from and going to the expo. Those arriving had come empty handed. Those departing carried white plastic bags (goodie bags, as they sometimes are called), the most important item in those bags being a bib, the number, that would allow them entry onto the starting grid for the 13.1-mile race they would run the next day: the OneAmerica 500 Festival Mini-Marathon, a.k.a. the Indianapolis Mini-Marathon, or the Indy Mini, or in its shortest form simply, the Mini. Gotta love any race that has a catchy nickname, so that as soon as it is spoken, everybody knows exactly what you're talking about. *The Mini!*

Thus on that Friday afternoon in May, arriving runners, I among them, turned left at the end of the corridor and walked through an archway festooned with the Mini's decorative logo. Passing through the archway, they found themselves in a new environment, a truly runner-friendly environment, as any runner who had attended a major race expo quickly would recognize. The Mini's expo occupied two joined rooms, Hall A and Hall B, crammed with booths and exhibits and a long line of tables where the preentered runners would pick up their goodie bags, all part of the ritual leading to their participation in the Mini.

But there is nothing miniature about the Mini, which is one of the largest half marathons in the United States, among the largest in the world, among the oldest races at the 13.1-mile distance, too. For 2015, approximately 25,000 had entered the 13.1-mile half marathon, another 4,000 had chosen the 5K (3.1 miles). (That added up to nearly 30,000 runners entered, although not all would appear for the race and finish.) I was entered in both races, having first filed my entry midwinter into the half marathon. Unfortunately, work on this book absorbed so much of my energy that I failed to get in as many long runs as planned. The longest was the 5 miles (8 km) I had run in the Winter Beach Run in Jacksonville Beach, Florida. If someone posting to my Facebook page had asked whether he or she could make the jump from 5 to 13.1 miles, I know what I would have replied. Just before leaving Florida to return home to Indiana, I filed a second entry, this one in the 5K. Luckily, the first and last miles of the 5K were the same as the first and last miles of the half marathon, allowing me to at least experience the flavor of the Mini, although missing the speedway lap in the middle.

Racers in the Indy Mini take their lap around the iconic Indianapolis Motor Speedway.
Courtesy of 500 Festival.

One of the appeals of the Mini, its unique feature, is a lap around the Indianapolis Motor Speedway, a 2.5-mile (4 km) lap around the iconic race track. The Mini course begins downtown, heads west to the speedway, then flows counterclockwise around the track, and finally returns east to downtown.

Certainly it is the lure of running on the speedway track that brings so many runners to Indianapolis the first weekend in May. But it is also the lure of the distance that has allowed the half marathon to pass even the marathon in popularity among runners not only in the United States, but also around the world. But where did the half marathon come from? What are its roots?

Popularity of the Half

Phil Stewart, editor and publisher of *Road Race Management*, discusses the popularity of the half marathon: "My theory is that the running world benefited greatly from the triathlon world, which popularized the distance Half Ironman as an event long enough to be perceived as noteworthy, but not so long as to be unattainable by the masses. The key fact is that this legitimized the term 'half.' Since the 'marathon' remains the peak distance in the running world, the half marathon absorbs that word, blends it with 'half,' and offers an event accessible to more people."

Roots of the Half

Trying to determine the history of the half marathon is no easy task. The marathon has a clearly established lineage, its beginning traced to the Battle of Marathon in 490 BC, the legendary run of the Greek warrior and messenger Pheidippides from the plain of Marathon into Athens. Legend has Pheidippides crying, "Rejoice, we conquer," then dying. Historians suggest that, attractive as it might be, the legend was at best, well, just a legend with few facts to back it up. Nevertheless, that did not prevent the organizers of the first modern Olympic Games in Athens in 1896 from adding a long-distance race of about 25 miles (or about 40 kilometers) to the track and field competition. A Greek shepherd named Spiridon Loues won that race, and the name "marathon" was forever imprinted on all future races of about that distance. In 1908, the organizers of the Olympic Games in London lengthened the marathon distance to 26 miles, 385 yards (or 42.195 kilometers) so that the Queen's grandchildren could see the start. For several years, the International Olympic Committee and International Association of Athletics Federations argued over the precise distance of a marathon. Boston did not switch to 26 miles, 385 yards until 1924. As late as 1946, the European Championships in Stockholm featured a marathon only 40.2 kilometers long. Eventually, everyone agreed that 26 and 385 were the proper numbers for full marathons.

Participation in half marathons has grown in popularity as the race distance is more accessible for more people.

Marathonfoto.com

But the Half?

Despite its tremendous current appeal, the half marathon can boast no equivalent history. The half has no myths. The half has no legends. No comrade in arms helped pace Pheidippides to the halfway point then slowed his pace and dropped out able to brag, "Hey, I got halfway. Credit me for inventing another event."

Nevertheless, the half marathon does possess a history of sorts. Although the Indy Mini ranks among the largest of American half marathons (trading the largest title lately with a newer half in Brooklyn, New York), it is not the oldest. That honor belongs to the Caesar Rodney Half Marathon in Wilmington, Delaware, begun in 1964, its name coming from one of the signers of the Declaration of Independence.

Some sources suggest the Lincoln Memorial Half Marathon in Springfield, Illinois, as the oldest American race at that distance. Indeed, Lincoln Memorial did begin a month earlier than Caesar Rodney on Abe Lincoln's birthday (February 12) in 1964. But its original distance was 12 miles, not 13.1 miles. The shift to the latter distance did not occur until the late 1970s, a time when half marathons first became popular and race directors saw the advantage in stabilizing distances.

Also, while discussing the subject of the half's historical origins, where should we place the Pikes Peak Ascent? Footraces to the top of that 14,414-foot (4,493 m) mountain date back to the 1920s. The Pikes Peak Marathon (up and down) got its start in 1952 with a separate race to the top sometimes held on a different day. Except the race to the top was not called a half, it was called an ascent. That was true about the name when I first ran the race in 1971, setting a masters record. Another variant is the distance, the length of the trail to the top measured 13.32 miles, and 7,815 feet (2,382 m) in terms of altitude gained. The Pikes Peak Ascent technically is not a half marathon, and it also is on a trail, not a road (if that makes any difference). Nevertheless, the Pikes Peak Ascent certainly deserves its place in half marathon history.

Statistician Ken Young, a past Pikes Peak Marathon champion, was among those who pioneered the certification of courses. Certification guarantees that if a race identifies itself as 13.1 miles, it has been properly measured as no less than that distance. Measurement usually is done by bicycle, a counter determining number of revolutions per mile or kilometer. USA Track & Field supervises certification of road courses, and while race directors can do it themselves, USATF strongly suggests they hire an experienced course certifier to guarantee the course measured is precisely the distance advertised.

Give to Caesar . . .

Young confirms Caesar Rodney as the first American half marathon (1964), and also identifies Route du Vin in Luxembourg and San Blas in Puerto Rico (both founded in 1966) as half marathons. Paderborner Osterlauf in Germany was run as a half marathon in 1954, but then was run at several other distances until resuming as a half in 1997. Young adds: "The South American Road Championships were held as half marathons as early as April 25, 1954, in São Paulo, Brazil. I would opine that 1954 marked the appearance of the half marathon as an official racing distance."

Tom Derderian, author of *Boston Marathon: The History of the World's Premier Running Event*, recalls several races in the 1970s as being about the half marathon distance: races in Holliston, Massachusetts, (13.7 miles) and Concord, New Hampshire, (13.5 miles). Neither event has survived, although Concord currently has a new race by the name of the Heads Up Half Marathon.

Andy Milroy, a British historian and statistician, explored half marathon history in the article, "The Origins of the Half Marathon," published in

The CR

Historically, the Boston Marathon, in April, can be linked to Paul Revere's ride to Lexington and Concord the night of April 18, 1775. The Caesar Rodney Half Marathon, known fondly by locals as the CR, is held annually in March and, dating from 1964, remains the oldest half marathon in the United States. It, too, can trace its roots to a patriot on horseback. Caesar Rodney in 1776 rode his horse 70 miles (113 km) from Delaware to Philadelphia, all night through a thunderstorm, so he could be present to vote for, and later sign, the Declaration of Independence.

An equestrian statue of Caesar Rodney now occupies Rodney Square in downtown Wilmington, the location of the finish line for the CR, whose first winner was Browning Ross of Woodbury, New Jersey, a two-time Olympian (1948, 1952), but perhaps more significantly, he was the founder of the Road Runners Club of America.

Only 33 runners ran the first CR Ross won with a time of 1:07:24, still impressive today given the hilly nature of the course. The winner in 2015 actually ran four minutes slower. The Delaware Track & Field Club (currently Delaware Sports Club) founded the Caesar Rodney Half Marathon, now managed by the American Lung Association in Delaware. The CR has remained small: 1,245 finishers in 2015, but so has the entry fee: $65. "It's a challenge for locals," says Doug White, who has run every CR since 1971. White admits that the hilly course probably scares away many new runners. "If you want a fast half time, you do the Philadelphia Distance Run."

The original Caesar Rodney certainly knew the way to Philadelphia, his 70-mile ride remaining a historic endurance event. Those entering the CR today know that they are following in the footsteps of Browning Ross, if not those of Caesar Rodney himself.

The Analytical Distance Runner, edited by Ken Young. Milroy identified a marathon on the British island of Guernsey in May 1909 where winner Charlie Gardiner, a professional runner, recorded 1:21:05 at the half marathon point, given in the newspaper as 13 miles, 200 yards. But that was his halfway split time, not an official finishing time.

Milroy also mentions the Morpeth-Newcastle race, held over the approximate distance of 13.6 miles (21.9 km) from 1904: "As late as 1960 in his book *Distance Running Records*, Road Runners Club statistician Dave Roberts describes it as '13 miles plus.' No mention is made of the race as a half marathon. Well into the 1980s in the RRC Newsletter, the race was still being describe as the Morpeth-Newcastle 13 1/2, or 13 5/8, not as a half marathon. Indeed, it had been listed as over 14 miles in the mid-1980s" (Milroy 2012).

The 13.1-mile distance, according to Milroy, found early favor in South America, a race that distance being held in Bogota, Colombia, as early as 1938, although later shortened slightly to 20 kilometers (12.4 miles). Argentina held a half in 1930. About the same time, there was a Fiestas Patrias Half Marathon in Lima, Peru, although not always 13.1 miles. (Milroy speculates that warm weather in South America dictated races shorter than 26.2 miles.) Australia had a half marathon as early as 1953: the Victorian Marathon Club's Half Marathon in the town of Moonee Valley.

The first European half marathon, Milroy suggests, was the Paderborn Road Race in 1954, but Milroy brands it as a one-off, the organizers experimenting with different distances. Young identifies the Paderborner Osterlauf (Easter Run), a half marathon that same year, later run at several distances, becoming a half marathon again in 1997.

"What seems to have been the first (lasting) half marathon in the UK," says Milroy, "was the Bernie Hames Memorial in September, 1957, 'over a distance of approximately half a marathon' with a three lap course that was accurately set at 13 miles 140 yards." In 1961, 1962, and 1963, Leonard (Buddy) Edelen, an American living in England, won the race. In 1963, Edelen broke the world record in the marathon with a time of 2:14:28 in the Polytechnic Marathon near London.

Milroy continues: "After a gap of perhaps 20 years after the standardization of the marathon at 42.195 kilometers in the early 1920s, races set at half that distance began to emerge, but it was not until the late 1950s that growth of such events really began. Why it took so long can only be surmised. During that period, many road races were point to point between cities and towns, and thus held over non-standard distances. Where standard distances were used, there was perhaps a preference for round numbers like 10 miles, 20 kilometers, 15 miles and 25 kilometers as opposed to 21.097 kilometers."

Those precise metric distances would fade from popularity as Ken Young notes: "The growth of the half marathon dried up participation at 20-K and 25-K as earlier races at these distances converted to the half marathon. In 1966, the combined number of performances in the Association of Road Racing Statisticians (ARRS) database for 20-K and 25-K was ten times that for the half marathon." By 1974, the half marathon surpassed the 20K. The big jump occurred from 1977 to 1978 when the number of half marathon performances more than doubled.

Not too coincidentally, those were the years when the Indy Mini arrived as a major race. In its first year, the Indy Mini was won by Frank Shorter, the 1972 Olympic marathon gold medalist. (Frank won the silver medal at the 1976 Olympics.) In the 1978 Mini, Bill Rodgers, four-time winner of the Boston and New York City marathons, won the race just ahead of Frank.

Running the Speedway

I am going to claim at least partial credit for founding the Mini—but only partial. Among the books I wrote is *Thirty Days in May*, about the 1969 Indianapolis 500 auto race won by Al Unser. While writing that book and several others about the motor sport, I had gotten to know many of the drivers, owners, and mechanics and organizers of the Indianapolis 500. The last several days before the auto race, I realized, cars remained in Gasoline Alley, not allowed to practice on the track. It occurred to me that the vacant 2.5-mile (4 km) track might offer a traffic-free venue for a road race, maybe even a marathon that would need to consist of 10 and a half laps. I approached the speedway owners with that idea, and at least they did not say no. In fact, they gave me permission to run on the vacant track.

Thus, several days before the 500 in 1974, I appeared at the track with a friend, Carl Carey, bent on testing the speedway for a marathon to be run the following May. We planned to run 20 miles (32.2 km), eight laps, but we had not anticipated the stress of running the turns banked at 9 degrees. Carl lasted seven laps. I went the full eight. Afterward, we both agreed that no way did we want to run that many laps on a track with four banked turns.

Two laps, however, might be doable, reasoned another friend, Chuck Koeppen, track and cross country coach at suburban Carmel High School. In 1975 and again in 1976, Koeppen organized a 5-mile (8 km) run at the speedway. The following year, the Indy Mini got its start with a single lap on the banked track, including the final mile of the race. Today, runners reach the speedway in the middle of their race. Flat aprons inside the banking make the turns much less stressful than what Carl and I had encountered.

Real Racing

Joe Henderson, author of numerous books including *Long Slow Distance*, recalls his first half marathon run in 1979, the Coronado Half in California. He now coaches runners in Eugene, Oregon, and, as with the national trend, notes a shift in numbers from the full to the half.

His feelings on the half as a racing distance are mixed: "It's a perfectly fine race with a terrible name. No other road running event is known as a portion of another. Nobody ever refers to the 5K as the half 10K. This gives the false impression that it's half of a marathon in training, pacing, and recovery. That's not entirely true.

"I'd prefer 20K races (double 10K?) to become the next big running trend, but that will never happen. The half should keep growing faster than the marathon, because for most of today's runners the 13.1 is where real racing ends. The marathon is more a survival test."

At the 2015 Indianapolis Mini-Marathon, Frank Shorter returned at age 66 to sign autographs at the expo, but also to run the race in a promotion billed as Faster than Frank. Finish in front of the Olympic champion, and the 500 Festival would donate $1 to one of several nonprofit organizations as part of the festival's "Mini with a Meaning" program. Shorter ran the half in 2:04:40; 6,025 participants ahead of him resulted in a $6,025 windfall for the nonprofits. (His winning time in 1977 had been an hour faster, 1:03:56.)

Frank Shorter had aged well, but so had the Mini. And the half marathon distance has exploded in its popularity all over the world.

3 | Ready to Run

Rebecca McPhail started to run at age 36. As McPhail tells the story, "The aim was just to be able to run for half an hour. If I was going to exercise, I wanted to spend at least that much time doing it. I remember feeling self-conscious, uncoordinated, slow, and the burning in my chest hurt. This was all in the first couple of minutes! But I was quite determined, so kept on doing my thing. Kept on reading. Kept on asking questions."

Questions. Questions. Everybody has questions. Beginners certainly have questions, but so do experienced runners.

McPhail continues: "The stumbling block was getting over the feeling that I didn't belong. My initial impression was that runners were those people who do marathons and train a lot harder than me. Surely, people running by me at supersonic speeds on the running paths must believe that I should not be there. I now know that other runners do not think that way. They are extremely supportive and are happy you are out the door and have your shoes on. It doesn't matter how fast or slow. I wish I had had a better understanding of that when I started. It's all about you and running your own race, not getting caught up in anyone else's goals as they go zooming by."

Caryn Festa, 37, a nurse anesthetist from Fayetteville, North Carolina, always had been a casual runner until she decided to train for a marathon. "I picked a race and picked a start date for my training. I had a 2-year-old and had to be at work at 6:30 a.m., so I knew I would need to run very early in the morning. The very first training day, I had 5 miles to run starting at 4:00 a.m. My sister agreed to listen to the baby monitor while I ran. My little girl never wakes up before 5:30, so I wasn't worried. Then as I was lacing up my shoes, she woke up. I tried to get her to go back to sleep, but she wanted no part of it.

"I knew if I didn't leave in the next five minutes I was going to miss my first day of training. I realized that over a period of months training for this race, I probably would need to skip a workout now and then, but it was very important to me that on the first day I get off to a good start, so I asked my daughter if she wanted to run with me in her stroller. Her face lit up, and she said, 'Yes!' My very first run was done in the pitch-black darkness with a safety strobe light and a flashlight tied to the handle of the stroller. She stayed awake and talked to me the entire run. My first run remains my favorite run, because it set the tone for my whole training. I was not letting anything get in my way."

So many runners remember that first run as a singular experience. "After my third child was born in 2012, I was able to quickly take off most of the baby weight through various forms of exercise other than running," writes Ashley Weingart, 37, a stay-at-home mom from Chagrin Falls, Ohio. (Weingart writes the blog *Running with Skissors*.) "When we went away on vacation, and I didn't have my elliptical machine, I decided to try going for a short jog down the beach—only a mile or two. I always had knee trouble, so running was usually out of the question, but I thought maybe the sand would be easier on the knees. I enjoyed that first run enough that when I got home from vacation, I began running more, and then more, and then some more after that. One year later I ran my first half marathon. I have since done four more halfs, plus the Big Sur Marathon Relay, where I ran 16 miles (25.7 km) and finally the Chicago Marathon, just missing my goal of 4 hours. My advice to new runners is this: Just

Getting Good Advice

Sarah Grabiec Rooks, 32, a title company branch manager from Chesapeake, Virginia, still admits to being a newbie. She had run a few 5Ks and was a few months from running her first marathon when she talked about what meant the most to her as a runner.

She said, "For years while in my 20s, I kept trying to run and failed. Self-doubt mainly plus some knee issues caused by a tight IT band. At age 31 I joined a gym and hired a personal trainer. She gave me the guidance I needed. The best advice she gave me was, 'Don't be afraid to walk.'

"She also told me to pay attention to what I ate, especially before a run, offering some suggestions for prerun snacks. My trainer also kicked my butt in strength training and recommended a foam roller, which improved my ITB issue. I can't afford to pay her all the time, but she was worth every penny my first three months of running consistently."

believe in yourself. You are capable of achieving so much more than you know. Let go of fear and seek 'the impossible.' You won't know if you can do it unless you try. You may just discover a new love and talent you didn't even know you had in you."

Good motivational advice, but while the Nike T-shirt motto to "Just do it!" still rings true, if you are an about-to-be new runner, or an already-begun-but-don't-know-what-I'm-doing runner, or even a bunch-of-half-marathons-on-my-résumé runner looking to boost your knowledge of the sport, let's take time to consider what runners need to know to participate regularly and enjoy the training leading up to a half marathon or any long-distance race.

Beginning Runner's Guide

In 1997, Amby Burfoot, an editor of *Runner's World*, asked me to write a *Beginning Runner's Guide* for the magazine's first venture onto the Internet. Much of the information contained in that guide (later published as a booklet) remains valid today. In the introduction, I wrote the following:

> Running is simple and inexpensive. It's a good way to lose weight. It makes you feel good. Running is good for your health. You'll look better and have more energy if you learn how to run (Higdon 1997, p. 1).

But how do you begin? That's a frequent theme for questions asked of me on the Internet. New runners want to know how to start. They want a training program. They want information about shoes and equipment. They worry about sore muscles.

Every runner experiences what might be described as start-up problems. Many have restart problems. Former runners (who stopped for one reason or another) want to get back to their old running routines. They too need help.

In that guide, I advised runners how to start—and how to restart. I'll save you the trouble of hunting for a copy online or in a bookstore. Here is a summary and update of what I wrote in that handy booklet long ago.

Physical Examination

Before you begin, it is a good idea to talk to your personal physician. Paul D. Thompson, MD, a cardiologist at Hartford Hospital in Connecticut, explains, "This is important if you have a family history of heart disease, if you are a current or former smoker, or if you are overweight." If you do not have a physician, get one now and ask for a general checkup. Many doctors will recommend an exercise stress test (usually done on a treadmill) to ensure that you have no cardiovascular problems, but this is not absolutely necessary if you are willing to start slowly and talk to your doctor if symptoms surface during training. "Stress tests detect established heart disease," says Dr. Thompson. "The rare heart problems that occur in runners often develop suddenly and are not detectable by those tests."

Despite the occasional death of people in road races, most often from a heart attack, but sometimes from miscellaneous medical reasons not always easy to detect, you probably are safer running 13.1 miles on a road with runners all around you and police holding back car traffic than driving on that same road with trucks and high-speed cars buzzing by.

Running is a benign form of exercise. Despite the stress we place on our bodies (perhaps because of that stress), runners have fewer heart attacks than sedentary people. We are redeemed by our healthy lifestyles.

Shoe Selection

"Don't waste your money on a new set of speakers," sang Billy Joel. "You get more mileage from a $79.95 pair of shoes advertised in *Runner's World*." Billy didn't sing the song exactly that way, so some updating seems necessary for today's market.

The single most important piece of equipment you must purchase as a runner is a pair of shoes. When I first published the *Beginning Running Guide*, I cavalierly suggested that a "cheap pair of sneakers" would suffice the first week or two. I wrote, "Just get out the door first, worry about equipment later." I'm not sure I still agree with myself.

That's because in the several decades since I wrote those words, there has been tremendous growth in the number of specialty running stores. These stores are owned and staffed by runners, who know the sport. They love serving beginners and know that if they help a new runner select the best possible pair of shoes (not necessarily the most expensive pair of shoes), that person will become a regular customer. As for brand, model, and price, any comments I might offer in this book would be immediately obsolete by the time you read them. Even *Runner's World* has a difficult time staying current with its shoe reviews. Shoe companies change what they are selling too frequently.

At First Place Sports, a store with a half-dozen branches in and around Jacksonville, Florida, sales staff use both treadmills and runs on the sidewalk outside the store to perform gait analysis on customers. "We normally begin by putting customers in a neutral shoe," says manager Simon O'Brien. "If that doesn't fit, we try different categories." First Place Sports stocks 60 to 70 styles each for women and men. "What we are looking for is the shoe that fits best for each individual customer," says O'Brien.

I recently contacted Bob Wischnia, a friend who currently works as a consultant for Mizuno in Austin, Texas. Previously, Wish supervised shoe reviews for *Runner's World* and certainly knows more about shoe selection than anyone I know. I asked Wish what runners (not merely new runners, but runners) should know before walking into a shoe store such as First Place Sports. His response was, "Just ask price range and what types of shoes (styles and models) are on sale. Then try on three or four of the suggested models and go for a short jog around the store or on a treadmill. Fit is the most important factor. Even a good shoe, if it fails to fit your feet, is worthless."

Clear your mind when it comes to shoe size, particularly if you are female. Sorry for being sexist, but women who stuff their feet into spiked shoes because it will make them look great at a cocktail party may need to go up a half size or more for running shoes. "Feet, particularly those of beginners, tend to swell the further you run," says Megan Leahy, DPM, a Chicago podiatrist. Hands swell as well because your cardiovascular system may not yet be up to the task of moving fluids from the extremities back toward the heart. Wish adds "There's no real secret to the shoe-selection process for a beginner, other than going to a reputable running store and placing your confidence in that store's shoe people."

The Foot of the Matter

Megan Leahy, DPM, a Chicago-area podiatrist, claims, "If runners are in the right shoes, they often don't need to see me." You can also avoid Dr. Leahy's services if you do not run too many miles in those shoes before shifting them to use only for weeding the garden. What should be the mileage limit? Dr. Leahy suggests 300 to 400 miles (483-644 km) a pair, although this can vary from runner to runner. Heavier runners wear out shoes faster; runners with what impolitely might be described as bad biomechanics also may need to stay on the short side of the prescribed number. "You can stretch the life of the shoes," suggests Dr. Leahy, "by switching between two pairs, allowing the shoes to rest and bounce back when not worn."

I've known Megan Leahy (now Megan Leahy Turnbull) since she came out for cross country as a ninth-grader at Elston High School in Michigan City, Indiana. I coached Megan for two years, then another coach took over, guiding her to a second-place finish at the Indiana High School State Championships, her team winning the title twice. Megan continued running at Indiana University, although a series of injuries limited her success. One reason she decided to become a podiatrist was to help runners avoid the injuries that plagued her. Leahy offers the following advice for runners, new and old, trying to select the best pair of shoes.

> I agree that it is very difficult to keep up on shoe models as they change frequently. Even when you believe you've found the perfect shoe, the next version may not be as ideal. That's why it is important to have a formal fitting at a specialty running shoe store.

continued

It's a good idea for runners to have a basic understanding of the different shoe types. Training shoes usually are divided into neutral, stability, and motion control. Neutral is the lightest, but also more cushioned and is appropriate for runners with high arches or supinated (rolling toward the outside) feet. Stability shoes work best for runners with mild flattening of the feet or mildly pronated (rolling toward the inside) feet. Lastly, motion control (structured, more rigid) is best for runners with very low arches and a pronated foot.

It gets a little dicey when you start putting body type into the mix. Someone who competes in the Clydesdale (heavyweight) division, yet still has a pretty normal foot type, or even a more highly arched foot, may still require a motion-control shoe because of girth.

Some runners can get away with a less structured or more neutral shoe if they add an orthotic or an insert. Another key to remember is that neutral shoes tend to wear out a little faster than more structured shoes, but this does not mean you should move up in stability just to avoid buying shoes as frequently. Terrain, stride, and body type all play a role in shoe wear as well. Some runners benefit from a lighter shoe or racing flat for speed and tempo work. This also extends the overall life of the shoes. However, not everybody can risk running in racing flats.

Dr. Leahy confesses that she gets injured whenever she attempts this. Even though she has a neutral foot type, neutral shoes are not for her. She continues:

Minimalist shoes are all the rage these days. I certainly have seen my share of injuries due to these shoes, but I do not see the countless runners who do well with them, as they don't end up in my office. Transitioning to lightweight shoes is best done slowly and preferably under the guidance of a podiatrist or physical therapist who understands running form.

Another key point regarding shoes is paying mind to the shoes you're wearing when you're *not* running. Many injuries can be traced back to dress shoes and everyday shoes. (In other words, beware of 4-inch (10 cm) spikes the night before or after your weekend long run.)

Shopping for running shoes should start with a gait analysis by the salesperson. This involves running on the sidewalk or store treadmill, wearing the various shoe options. Well-fitted shoes should feel comfortable as soon as they're donned. Do not hope you can break them in. That being said, do not run a long run or race in a new pair of shoes. Ease into them with walks around the house and shorter runs. Most reputable shoe stores will accept returns and exchanges even if the shoe shows slight wear. Be sure to ask about return policies before you buy!

Do not feel as though you are married to your shoe size. Everyone's feet expand with age, and there is considerable variability of shoe sizes between brands and even within shoe brands. Toenail problems can often be traced back to a too-short or too-narrow shoe. Sometimes it's best to have a dedicated long-run shoe that is half a size bigger than your other workout shoes.

Local running friends are often savvy as to which running shoe stores are best in the area. Unless you are buying an identical version of a previous shoe, it is best not to shop online. If you wear orthotics, be sure to take them for your fitting. Make sure you block out plenty of time in your schedule for that fitting, and it's always best to shop for shoes at the end of the day when your feet are at their biggest.

Be sure to examine the shoes for defects. Place the shoes side by side on a table and view the heels from behind. The shoes should not tilt to the right or left and should be a mirror image of each other.

Megan offers a last word of advice: "Do not buy shoes based on their color!"

Running Attire

When I first started running—in high school and continuing into college—the word attire did not exist. Well, maybe you could find the word attire in your dictionary, which was on a shelf rather than in your computer, but nobody would have connected the word attire with what we wore at practice and in races at Carleton College. Arriving at the locker room each afternoon at 4:00, I would change into my running clothes, which consisted of a jock strap, a pair of white shorts, and a white cotton T-shirt emblazoned on the chest with "Property of Carleton College," which guaranteed that all of us on the team would make that T-shirt our property because of the status it offered us walking from class to class.

For cold days we wore gray sweat suits: baggy bottoms and loose-fitting tops. I don't recall the school providing us with much more in the way of attire, so we survived the Minnesota winters by layering more clothing, including parkas made of a material normally used for U.S. Army tents. A pair of undershorts over the jock strap or even a wool sock stuffed in the right place also protected our manhood. Nobody on our team froze, as far as I can remember, but we usually finished outdoor runs in the winter soaked with sweat and covered by frost. If continuing to run outdoors between cross country and track seasons was uncomfortable, why do I have such pleasant memories of those winter workouts?

That was in the 1950s, and even in the 1960s as I continued my running career postcollegiate, athletic clothing had not improved much. There were too few road runners to attract the attention of attire manufacturers. My best marathon came at Boston in 1964 on a wet and cold day where, in order to stay warm, I wore under my racing singlet a cotton turtleneck that certainly weighed an extra pound or more before I turned toward the finish line, then on Exeter Street. Did the weight of the soggy clothing add minutes to my time? Possibly, but every other runner in the race faced the same handicap. This is certainly one reason why our finishing times back then look so feeble compared to times today. Or that's my rationale.

Then in the 1970s and through the 1980s and the 1990s and now into the new millennium, road running emerged as a mainstream sport, attracting not merely more runners (female as well as male), but more merchants who discovered that servicing those runners could work to their financial benefit. No criticism implied: I love not being forced to wear cumbersome clothing, either in training or in races. You, too, can take advantage of all the attire available to us.

While you are in the specialty running store purchasing your first pair of running shoes, check out the clothing, the attire: shorts, singlets, sports bras, all made out of wicking materials in bright colors and trendy fashions. You don't need to make a purchase immediately. Shoe box under your arm, you can walk away without further damaging your bank account, because for your first steps as a walker, jogger, or runner, you can grab almost anything out of your clothing drawers. After a few weeks or months running, you probably will want to look good as well as feel good. Treat yourself. Buy the color-coordinated gear that makes you feel like a supermodel on the cover of *Vanity Fair*.

Jane Alred, owner of First Place Sports, suggests, "As far as apparel goes, a well-fitting bra is very important for women. Socks also are key to a runner's comfort, and moisture-wicking apparel is a must. Technology has improved greatly in recent years. Much of the apparel now on the market has thermo-regulating and odor-preventing properties. Tights and capris are popular now, and this serves to support muscles well. Compression is another category."

The best way to learn about clothing is to go to a road race, the equivalent of going to the Detroit Auto Show if you want to learn about fast cars. You do not even need to run the race; simply attend a 5K or 10K to observe. Or a half marathon or marathon—the more runners entered, the better—where you will see the widest and wildest collection of fashionable and unfashionable clothes.

It's important to choose the clothes most comfortable for you. No matter what you're wearing, you'll still feel like a superhero when you finish your half marathon.
Marathonfoto.com

The first thing you will notice is that nobody cares what anybody else looks like. You can look svelte or you can look sloppy. It is almost impossible to make a fashion faux pas. Almost impossible, but not totally impossible. A few picky veterans feel that you should not wear the race T-shirt in the race itself. Supposedly, this brands you as a rookie. It would be more an error if that shirt were cotton rather than a more comfortable wicking material. Cotton is okay for short, midweek runs, but for a 13.1-mile race (and for long workouts), cotton gets soggy and heavy and causes chafing.

In an Internet survey I took of runners who followed me online, runners favored comfort far ahead of fashion when it came to picking clothes. Far ahead! Use workouts, particularly long workouts, to experiment with your own personal clothing choices.

When it comes to those choices, the most important word is "layering." Begin with the almost bare basics—a pair of shorts or tights. Popular among women lately are shorts that look like skirts. Many male runners enjoy running bare-chested during the hottest of summer days; as for women, the word "minimalist" works for clothing items other than minimalist shoes.

But in choosing what to wear and what not to wear, consider that the sun overhead often can be more of a problem than the heat. A loose T-shirt can protect against sunburn as can suntan lotion, particularly a product with a high SPF number. Also, if you do a lot of running beneath a burning sun, wear a loose cap to protect your face and sunglasses to protect your eyes. Will this make you look dorky? Joan Benoit Samuelson won the 1984 Olympic Marathon wearing a cap that very much was dorky, so do you really care how you look?

When temperatures drop, the layering begins. Now you do need that T-shirt—and maybe a long-sleeve shirt over that. Every clothing item should be made of a wicking fabric that will pass moisture (your sweat) up and out. What will keep you warm in winter is not only the fabric, but also the air trapped between fabric. Continue layering for comfort, understanding at the same time that the more clothes you wear, the slower you will become. Do not try to compare your split times on a cool day in October with those on a cold day in January or, for that matter, on a hot day in May.

In cold weather, substitute a wool cap for the dorky cap, perhaps with a balaclava mask that will minimize bare skin exposure in cold winds. The wool cap will help retain warm air from rising and departing the body. Also important is keeping the extremities warm. Layer your hands, too, keeping in mind the fact that mittens will keep those hands warmer than finger gloves. For the coldest winter workouts, I wore woolen mittens as my first layer with leather mittens as the top layer. I never had a problem keeping my feet warm. A single pair of socks usually worked for me, but that may not be enough for you. As with all items of clothing, experiment to see what works for you. Of course, if you plan to spend the months of winter running only on an indoor treadmill, all of the above may be lost on you. Fair enough, but as an expatriate Minnesotan, I remember those days running in subzero weather as being exhilarating. Some of the fastest American marathoners have come from Minnesota and other cold-weather states. That includes Buddy Edelen, who set a world record for the marathon in 1963, and Janis Klecker, winner of the 1992 Olympic Trials marathon.

As for other equipment, sometimes I feel that my simple little sport of running has become overwhelmed with equipment. Is there a single gadget that every runner should own? First Place Sports' Simon O'Brien identifies GPS watches as their most popular electronic device. GPS watches allow runners to measure time, distance, pace, and much more. Personally, I love my app on my iPhone, which allows me to view a map of the route just run after I return home. It confirms the fact that, yes, I ran that course. Depending on how many bells and whistles you want on your watch, you can spend between $100 and $500. Another best-selling item, says O'Brien, is foam rollers. Nothing electronic about them, but you can rub the rollers along a sore or injured muscle and recover more rapidly.

Sore Muscles

Yes, you are going to suffer sore muscles when you begin. Stop! Don't throw your new running shoes into the back of your closet. It's not your fault. "No matter how fit you may be from other physical activities," I wrote in the *Beginning Running Guide*, "when you begin to run you're probably going to experience sore muscles." Even after running becomes easy, you will still experience sore muscles from time to time. People get sore muscles for three reasons:

1. They are not used to exercising.
2. They are used to a different exercise.
3. They push their regular exercise too hard.

Scientists say soreness starts as a result of tiny tears in the muscle fibers similar to a paper cut on your finger. (It hurts, but you can still use the finger.) What happens next is that the body's defense mechanism kicks in, white cells come to the rescue, and fluid moves into spaces it normally does not occupy, resulting in swelling. This normal swelling nudges the nerve endings, causing soreness. It also contributes to stiffness in the muscles, partially immobilizing them, as a cast might immobilize a broken arm or leg. The body does not want its injured part to move, or at least not move too much. Swelling and soreness often peak 48 hours after exercise, one reason why your muscles hurt more the second day.

Usually when I schedule a massage, I do so in a window (24 to 72 hours) after a planned hard workout, most often after a weekend long run. Monday is my massage day, and if you examine most of my training programs—particularly for novice runners—you will discover that Monday usually is a rest day with no running programmed. However, Friday also is a rest day, and getting a relaxing massage in advance of a hard workout also is a good idea. Paraphrasing Will Rogers, I never met a massage I didn't like. If I were still functioning at the elite level, where my annual income depended upon my ability to win races, I probably would schedule a massage three to five days a week. I would also regularly use a physical therapist as well as a massage therapist. I probably also would have podiatrist Megan Leahy, who I coached in high school, on retainer. The minute even the slightest muscle twitch materialized, I would be texting Megan for preventative advice. Most of us weekend warriors do not have this luxury. We need to learn how to avoid injuries that will both take us away from our training and cost money. The way to do that is to learn to function well beneath the pain level.

Pain is good and not bad. It is a warning signal to back off training. Not every runner knows how, or wants to know how, to avoid pain. Often we practice denial, not willing to admit that a hurt may become a permanent hurt unless we treat it, which may mean to stop running. No, we would not do that! A general rule is that if pain comes at the start of a workout, but gradually diminishes as your muscles warm, keep going. But if pain gets worse as you run, causing you to become a limper rather than a runner, it is time to stop and seek medical care.

In other words, know when to stop. Whether or not it is bad for your ego, shift from running mode to walking mode. If the pain persists, halt. If the problem is more muscle fatigue than a developing injury, the pain should begin to retreat. Stretching the muscle may or may not help, and I am inclined to not recommend specific stretching exercises, because if you overstretch, you can cause more problems than you cure. Once the pain has begun to disappear, you should be able to begin walking, then jogging, then running again. Hopefully, you can finish the workout. Aches and pains are part of any new sport a person tries, and that certainly includes running. Let me add that I am not in favor of pain-killing medications, particularly ibuprofen, which has some troubling side effects if used too often or in too high doses.

But don't feel guilty if pain seems a problem. The important message to take home from this discussion—particularly if you are a novice—is that you are not alone. All runners experience soreness, particularly when they have run hard or run far. It's part of training. You rest. You recover. After your muscles recover, they actually should be stronger. Forcing your muscles to move the body in a horizontal plane is what gets you in shape. One way to avoid sore muscles is to not do too much too soon. Gentle training will get you to the finish line of a half marathon or any other race distance you choose.

Where and When

The question of where and when to run seems easy to answer: anywhere and at any time. But for a beginner setting out on his or her first journey, the answer may not seem quite that obvious. Most beginners start by running around the block or down the street in their neighborhoods. Only later, do they seek varied locations for their running activities. Here are some points to consider about where to run.

Roads

The name of the sport is road running. Most races are run on roads. Most training also takes part on roads, mainly for convenience. But there are perils on the roads because of the mean looking vehicles occupying them. When possible, run in low-traffic areas. Dodging cars is not fun. Run facing traffic so you can see cars coming at you in your lane and step aside to avoid getting clipped. Don't assume the driver, who may be texting or talking on a cell phone, will see you. When I see runners running with traffic, I immediately think "rookie" and hope that they soon realize that almost every other runner is on the other side of the road. My wife once tried to tell a lady who was running with traffic that she should move to the other side of the road. The woman snapped at her, "Sez who?" Sez me; that's the answer.

Paths

Many cities have parks with paths and sidewalks designated for endurance athletes (and this can include walkers, cyclists, and skaters). Chicago has an 18-mile (29 km) lakefront. New York has a mile-and-a-half (2.4 km) loop around the Central Park Reservoir. Usually these are pleasant places to run because you can avoid automotive traffic. Plan to do at least some of your running on popular paths. The best ones feature toilets, water fountains, and even mile markers. If you ever run past my home on Lake Shore Drive in Long Beach, Indiana, I have a water fountain out front for the benefit of the many runners and other fitness athletes. The water bears mystical properties as befitting the fountain of a running guru. Drink from it, and you will nibble seconds, maybe minutes, from your next half marathon time.

Many half marathon courses offer scenic routes through parks and trails.

Cross Country

Once you develop an ability to run 3 to 4 miles (4.8-6.4 km) nonstop, consider heading into the woods. Uneven ground may seem difficult at first, but running on soft (rather than hard) surfaces can help prevent injuries. The ideal running surface is smooth grass, such as on a golf course, but golfers often object to runners on their turf. My favorite running areas include the twisting trails of Indiana Dunes State Park in the summer and the flat and hard sand of Ponte Vedra Beach where we spend winter months. At low tide, the surface is perfect, and the scenery is not bad either. I actually believe that running on uneven surfaces protects you against injury, because it forces you to adapt to different foot plants. Once while running in the Indiana Dunes State Park with the high school cross country team I coached, I saw the ankle of the girl in front of me bend at what seemed like a 90-degree angle. Fearing serious damage, I expected the team might need to carry her off the trail and head to a hospital. She just kept running. Her ligaments and muscles apparently were so strong from our frequent trail runs that she had arrived at a level where runners often are able to minimize, if not prevent, injuries. I probably should concede that she was only 15 years old. Youth has its advantages.

Track

My first run was on the running track at the University of Chicago, as an athlete at the university's high school. One advantage of tracks is that almost all are exactly 400 meters long, meaning four laps equal 1,600 meters, approximately a mile. You will know exactly how far you run each workout provided you know how to count, although GPS watches will not accurately track someone running in circles. Tracks are great for doing speed work, the interval training that I prescribe for advanced runners. Tracks provide privacy and, also, because running is the main reason people go to tracks, they offer the opportunity to tap into psychological support.

I used to love to work out on Wednesday evenings at the Bolles High School track in Jacksonville, Florida, for just that reason. One problem is that some high schools, unlike Bolles, close their tracks to the public. Maybe athletic directors are worried that some delinquent might steal a high hurdle. The University of Chicago's Stagg Field was in what once might have been described as a tough part of town, although that neighborhood has been gentrified lately. When asked about locking the track each night, Coach Ted Haydon told the athletic director that he would rather have the neighborhood kids feel they were welcome inside rather than keeping them outside, since they would be less likely to create mischief. I have hopped the fence many times to use our local track in my hometown, although don't hold me liable if you get injured doing the same.

When

When to run? Any time still holds as an answer, but most runners start their day with a morning workout. This wakes them up and guarantees that they will get in their run that day and not have work or unexpected family obligations derail their training plans. When the late Jim Fixx was promoting *The Complete Book of Running*, being taken from interview to interview in a limousine because the book was a bestseller, I drove into Chicago to appear on a TV program with him and Erma Tranter, then director of the Chicago Area Runners Association. After the show, Jim had extra time so we headed over to her house (Jim in his limousine) to go for a run together.

During the run, I mentioned that this was my second workout, I had gotten up at something like 4:00 a.m. so I could get my miles in before driving into Chicago. Erma was astounded because she always ran in the evening, squeezing the run in before dinner or sometimes running after dinner in the dark with a too-full stomach. After our talk, she switched to morning running, hating it at first, loving it later, because it opened up evenings for family activities.

In the middle of summer, you can avoid the heat of the day by running early, although in the middle of winter, I used to run at noon to absorb as much warmth as I could from an overhead sun. Fortunately, being a freelance writer with an office in my home, I could run at any time of day I wanted. Not everybody has that luxury, although flexible hours are a lot more common now than when I was training twice daily.

I must confess that I hate Daylight Saving Time. Just as winter fades enough so that morning runners begin to see the sun, the Clock Gods trick us and steal our hour and give it to those who inhabit the night. Very unfair. If I could undo any one facet of 21st century life, it would be Daylight Saving Time.

In an ideal world, we should be able to run anywhere at any time without fear of being assaulted. Our world is not ideal, so be careful where you train and when you train. If you have to run in the dark or in unpatrolled areas, it's generally safer to do so in the early morning rather than in the evening. When possible, train with a partner. Everyone should run defensively. This may mean not wearing headphones because this will make you less aware of danger signals.

Finally, if running in the dark, please do so wearing a reflective vest so drivers can see you from in front and behind. Every now and then, I will see some runner—no insult meant, but most often a young runner—pass in the dark wearing dark clothes and, it gets worse, on the right (incorrect) side of the road. Oh, my gosh, I think, if you want to commit suicide why not instead swim out into a shark-infested ocean?

Running Lifestyle

Sharks aside, in deciding to run a half marathon, you made a very important choice that will extend your lifespan, as underlined by Dr. Kenneth H. Cooper, author of the best-selling *Aerobics*. He said, "Our research suggests that people who exercise regularly can extend their lifespan by six to nine years."

Ken made that comment to me when I visited with him in his office after a physical exam at the Cooper Institute in Dallas. That statement seemed so startlingly off the top that I asked Dr. Cooper to repeat it. *Six to nine years of extra life. Did I correctly hear what Ken had said?* Yes, I did, and he had nearly a half century's worth of data from tens of thousands of his own patients and members of the center to back up that statement.

"More important," said Dr. Cooper, "people who exercise improve their *quality* of life." The health benefits kick in once you achieve a regular routine of exercising at least every other day for 30 to 60 minutes. For runners, this means 10 to 15 miles (16-24 km) a week. You will achieve that in week 1 of my 12-week half marathon program. That's where you begin. Training for a half marathon, you certainly will run more than that in a week. At peak training, if you follow one of my more advanced schedules, you will run that much in a single day. Yes, you will, although what counts most is what you do after running 13.1 miles in a single race, what you do in the next weeks, in the next months, in the next years. Here's the plan: Make regular exercise part of your lifestyle to obtain the benefits promised you by Dr. Cooper. You'll look better. You'll feel better. You'll live longer. That's what Ken promises, and let me double down on his remarks.

It's not merely the running, but also all of the activities that accompany the running lifestyle. You eat better. You lose weight. If you smoke, you probably will kick that habit as soon as you realize that smoking considerably affects your performance. Plus nobody in your new peer group smokes. Nobody! Or if they do, they hide that habit carefully. If you drink, you'll probably limit yourself to a single beer while watching football on TV or a single glass of wine while chomping down on a plate of spaghetti, a.k.a., pasta. I have an Italian American wife; she certainly has contributed to my longevity. Long before there was a Mediterranean diet promoted in best-seller books, I benefitted from that diet, and so will you. Also, you won't hang out in the bars past midnight if you know there is a long run scheduled the next morning in your training for a half marathon. Priorities suddenly change when there is bling to be collected at the end of the training tunnel.

One warning as we move forward in the next chapter to the subject of training: Running is addictive. Once you get started, you may find you no longer want to give it up. But it is a positive addiction with tremendous benefits. You will thank yourself (and me) that you decided to train for a half marathon.

4 | First Steps

Many who consider themselves lifetime runners, who now love running with a passion, who have finished numerous half marathons and races at other distances, who have qualified for and run the iconic Boston Marathon, suffered painful beginnings.

I'm not going to hide the reality of our sport: Running sometimes hurts. It can hurt if you're a beginner, but it also can hurt if you are an experienced runner. It can hurt at the start of a workout when you are not properly warmed up. It can hurt in the middle of a workout, if you chose a pace too fast for the planned distance. It can hurt at the end, particularly at the end of a road race (your first or your 762nd) as you push to nibble a few seconds more off your finishing time. And sometimes it can hurt for several days after a hard workout or race where you pushed yourself to the limit. Running 13.1 miles, no matter how fast or slow, might be considered as pushing to the limit.

Consider Jeff Stoward, 47, a management consultant from Brisbane, Australia. Jeff confesses that over a bottle of red wine he accepted a dare to sign up for an Olympic-distance triathlon, never having run a step in his life. (For those unfamiliar with triathlon terminology, the Olympic-distance features a 1.5K [.93 mile] swim, a 40K [25 miles] bike ride, and a 10K run.) The next morning after the sign-up, Stoward decided to test his ability to run the 10K leg. "I couldn't walk for five days," groans the now wiser Australian.

April Moorehead, 45, a teacher from Rochelle, Illinois, began somewhat more wisely, running for 60 seconds, walking for 60 seconds, then running for 60 seconds more. "I will never forget how excruciatingly impossible

60 seconds of solid running felt," Moorehead recalls. "I did not feel I deserved to call myself a runner. The journey was gradual. Throughout the journey, I learned those one-minute intervals did qualify me as a runner. I now compare myself to no one but myself. I watched myself evolve. Now, my battle is the last 60 seconds of a half marathon."

Julie Lake, 46, a personal trainer from Bay City, Michigan, remembers not even being able to make it around her block: "I had to walk and catch my breath. It felt horrible, but I was determined to make the entire block running. Once I did that, I felt an amazing sense of accomplishment." Darren Croton of Wanganui, New Zealand, sums up his first day of running succinctly: "My lungs said ouch."

Nobody says running is easy. Do you remember me making that remark? I don't think so. Go back and reread the first few chapters. Most difficult are those first few steps on that first day, the day when you embrace a new lifestyle, the day when you decide to become a runner.

How you begin depends partly on your current level of fitness. Teenagers, or people already in good shape from participation in other sports, might have little trouble running a mile or two (1.6-3.2 km) the first day. They might be stiff and sore the second or third day, but they will have made a beginning. Someone unused to exercise might struggle to walk even a mile. People carrying a few extra pounds might find themselves struggling to get from their driveway to the neighbor's driveway.

Janet Hamilton, 53, a nurse from Woodland, California, never considered herself athletic. "I was never a runner until age 49," she says. Then a friend suggested they run a half marathon together. Hamilton said, yes, figuring she could back out. Then she overheard her 20-year-old daughter say to her father, "I don't think mom can do this." That proved to be a motivational moment.

Hamilton left the house the next morning for what she planned as a 1-mile (1.6 km) run. She recalls, "I got about two blocks from home and wanted to stop running, but there were a bunch of guys putting a roof on a house. I desperately wanted to walk, but I wouldn't stop running because they were watching. So I kept running to the turnaround point, a half mile (800 m), and really wanted to walk back home. But once again, I didn't want these guys to see me walking, so I kept running and made it home. I ran my first half marathon six months later. After crossing that finish line, the feelings of accomplishment, strength, and invincibility were incredible and changed me as a person. Since then, I've run 15 half marathons. And now, I run for me, not those guys on the roof."

Guys on the roof probably know little about proper running form. They are not likely to sit on their shingles and, like judges in a gymnastics or figure skating competition, give you a score signifying your success as a smooth runner.

Looking Good

Before you begin, what do you need to know about good running form? Not much. I'm inclined to tell you, just go out and run and don't worry whether or not you look good as a runner. One cheer that spectators often shout to runners passing in half marathons is, "Looking good!" I would say the same, except I know that many new runners do agonize over form. "Am I doing it right?" is a common worry, not only among beginners, but also among seasoned veterans. Particularly among the latter is the feeling that if they worked on their form, perhaps under the supervision of a good coach, they might be able to nibble a few seconds, maybe more than a few seconds, off their personal records (PRs).

Those seasoned veterans are right. When it comes to running form, here are a few areas to consider, based on my own experiences plus those of Coach Roy Benson from Amelia Island in Florida.

Maintain a Heads-Up Attitude

Keep your head up, focused on the road 10 to 20 meters ahead of you. Don't let your chin drop so you are looking down at your feet. This is a sign of defeat. Admittedly, it is tough to stay focused, particularly in the closing miles of a half marathon, particularly slogging up steep hills. Assuming a heads-up attitude will help you maintain both running form and speed. Don't let your form deteriorate in the closing miles; it will slow you down.

Hold Arms Midbody

Don't carry your arms too high or too low. Your arms should bend 90 degrees at the elbow. When you swing your arms, you do not want your elbows pinned too tightly against your side. Instead, says Coach Benson, let them swing back and forth along your side to the front of your ribs. Beware of excessive arm swing! You can control this by not allowing your hands to cross your body's midline (chin to belly button). Keep the back of the wrists within an inch or two of your singlet during the entire arm swing. It will be easier to do this (and thus keep your shoulder muscles relaxed), if you rotate your hands, wrists, and forearms slightly (thumbs inward), about 45 degrees off the thumbs-up position.

Swing Away

Everyone has a slightly different arm swing. I swing my arms near my waist almost as though I am scratching my belly. Try this, and see if you feel comfortable as a Hal look-alike. Otherwise, relax and see what works for you—particularly at the end of a hard workout. Relax your hands; don't clench your fists, which will tighten your entire body. Sometimes you will notice runners lower their arms and shake their hands at the wrist to aid relaxation. This is not a bad fix for tightness as long as you are not forced to do it too often.

Running with proper form is very important. You should remain upright with arms close to the middle of your body. Do not overstride.

Marathonfoto.com

Stay Close to Vertical

Runners in motion sometimes look like they're leaning forward, but this is not true. At least it's not true for runners who possess good form. This includes sprinters running distances as short as 200 and 400 meters. Sprinters start in blocks and rise gradually to vertical, but once they reach that straight-up position, they stay vertical at least until it comes time to dive across the finish line. Straight up remains the best posture also for half marathoners, even going up steep hills. Maybe *especially* going up those hills. Ignore anyone on the sidelines who tells you to "lean into it." They mean well, but they're flat-out wrong, Coach Roy Benson forcefully told me: "Assuming a heads-up attitude will help you maintain both running form and speed."

Do Not Overstride

Having a long stride seemingly should allow you to cover more ground more efficiently. This is not necessarily true. For many runners, and especially distance runners, a short but quick stride often is more economical. Here's a guarantee from both Roy and me: Improve economy, and you will run faster. Scientists identify 180 strides per second as the most economical pace. It may be for many runners, although maybe not for you. At least until after you have been running a while, don't get hung up in counting cadence or changing your pace to achieve a magic 180. A runner who was 6 feet, 4 inches (1.9 m) asked me on Facebook whether he should try lengthening his stride. Maybe, maybe not, I told him. "Run at whatever cadence feels comfortable for another year, then ask me again. You probably will already know the answer."

Run in a Straight Line

This advice seems almost too obvious, but I sometimes find myself running behind runners who wander back and forth across the road, not realizing that they are adding extra yards (or meters) to their journey. This happened to me once in a road race where I found myself trailing a friend, a talented runner but one who wandered back and forth from side to side of the road so much you would think he was drunk. I hung well behind him most of the way to avoid getting dizzy and eventually passed him in the final sprint to the finish. When I mentioned this form fault to my friend, he admitted to not knowing how much he wandered. His problem was a lack of concentration, but you can teach yourself to run in a straight line by running down the painted line in the middle of a road. (Make sure it is a low-traffic road.) Even better, practice straight-line running at a track with clearly marked lanes. In races, look far down the road to determine whether the course will turn left or right. Cutting a straight-line tangent to the inside curb may allow you also to cut a few tenths of a second off your finishing time. Tenths add up over a 13.1-mile race.

Don't Overthink Foot Placement

It is difficult to determine the exact point at which the foot strikes the ground. Most fast runners—even the sprinters—probably land midfoot, settle onto the heel, then push off from the ball of the foot. But at 180 steps a minute, even the sharpest scientists and coaches probably need a slo-mo camera to analyze foot strike. Most runners in the middle of the pack probably land heel first, but only slightly because this all happens so fast. At some point in your running career, you may want to step onto a treadmill and have a knowledgeable coach like Roy Benson tell you exactly what is happening from the ankle down. Otherwise, don't worry about it.

Observe Good Form in Other Runners

Here are three more quick tips.

1. *Tune into televised track and field meets or road races.* How do the fastest of the fastest look? Mimic them.

2. *Hand your iPhone to a friend and have him or her record you running.* You don't need to post it on YouTube to determine your own efficiency.

3. *Seek the advice of a coach.* This is always a good idea (if you can afford individual coaching). A coach may be able to fine-tune your form.

New Year's Resolution

January is always a peak month for sign-ups for my online programs. Either immediately before or after January 1, a lot of people—often new runners—make a resolution: I'm going to run a half marathon.

It's easy to make a resolution with champagne bubbles in your eyes on New Year's Eve. But will you be able to fulfill your bargain with the devil the following spring or fall, depending on which race of 13.1 miles you place on your bucket list? Before mailing in your entry blank, consider some questions that may affect your success.

1. **Evaluate your fitness.** Yes, your friends are planning to run a half, and you want to join them, or there is a cause for which you want to raise money, charity running being one of the major motivators for half marathon runners, but stop! Is this a realistic goal? If you are overweight and want to use a half marathon to lose pounds, maybe you should lose those pounds *before* embarking on a training program. If you are young and fit because you play soccer or ride a bike to work like our granddaughter Angela (7 miles each way), no problem. If over 35 with a family history of heart disease and an addiction for watching ESPN with beer and popcorn by your side, you might want to consult a doctor and get a physical exam before punching the go button.

2. **Pick an interim goal.** If starting from a low level of fitness, that goal might be to run a single mile without stopping—or even to walk that mile. Most cities have 5K races where the entry fees are less than $25 compared to the $100 or more you might pay for a major half marathon in the United States. Test your ability first in a 5K or 10K. Even though Running USA confirms that approximately four times as many runners ran half marathons in 2014 than full marathons, the ubiquitous 5K tops them both in numbers. Short-distance races make great interim goals for those planning to eventually run half marathons.

3. **Do you have time?** What else in your busy life is liable to conflict with your half marathon plans? Most half marathon training programs prescribe long runs that may take you several hours to complete on weekends and several hours more to recover. They also often require midweek runs that may require getting up at 5:00 a.m. to run before going to work. Studying for a law exam? Taking care of several young kids? Just moved into a new house or fixing up an old one? Is this a good year for running your first half marathon, or is that a bucket list item that can be postponed until your work and family schedule provides you with more recreational time?

4. **Select a good training program.** This is a self-serving statement because I offer a half dozen 12-week training programs for the half

marathon on my website, plus programs for other distances: 5K to full marathon. Advertisement aside, you do not—repeat *not*—want to enter into this important commitment flying blind. Use the experiences of those who have gone before you. Running is perhaps the simplest sport. You simply put one foot in front of the other and move. You don't have to kick a ball; you don't have to swing a racket. But it takes planning to build your body up to a level where you can run 13.1 miles. Let a good coach do the planning for you, even if you only see that coach online.

5. **Build a support team.** Yes, running is an individual sport, but you'll achieve greater success if the people around you—your family and friends—know what you're doing. You very definitely need the support of your spouse, particularly if there are childcare issues that need resolution. Determine a schedule for the two of you. If you borrow three hours from family activities on a weekend, give back three hours or more at another time. Sit down with your support team before week 1 of training to make sure each of you knows what to expect.

Do all that and your half marathon dream can become a reality. All you need to do now is start to run.

Barefoot Running

What about so-called minimalist shoes? The best-selling book *Born to Run* by Christopher McDougall created a lot of hype about barefoot running. To achieve nirvana, it suggested, we had to shed our heavier-than-needed training shoes and run free across various landscapes, including sand, grass, and even asphalt and concrete. I speak to you as someone who has run barefoot for half a century, beginning when I caught a case of athlete's foot so bad it forced me to throw away my infected shoes and run barefoot on the grass inside the track at the University of Chicago's Stagg Field for nearly a full summer. I loved running bare, so from that point on, I continued to run barefoot on the grass fairways of golf courses and on beaches, the best being Ponte Vedra Beach, Florida.

But as a barefoot runner, I very much am in the minority. One of my favorite races is the Winter Beach Run in Jacksonville Beach, 5-mile (8 km) and 10-mile (16 km) races at low tide on a firm but bouncy surface. But checking the feet of the approximately 800 runners in that race recently, I spotted only a handful of us running barefoot. So, yes, give barefoot running a try, but only on appropriate surfaces, otherwise your next medical visit will be to a podiatrist.

Having said that, my fellow author Christopher McDougall may be onto something when it comes to wearing minimalist shoes, particularly in road races where you go hunting for a PR. The best advice is to run (or at least race) in the lightest pair of shoes you can use without getting injured. Because I possess good biomechanics, my shoe of choice for most fast workouts is one halfway between heavy training and light racing flats, but I have multiple pairs of shoes in my closet, and that is probably true of most people who have been running two years or more.

Still, you can't begin to think about shoe choice if you are not yet running. There is no perfect form for standing stationary. It is time to begin: Start running. Or maybe even start walking before committing yourself to the bouncier running stride. Whichever, the key ingredient is not a fancy pair of shoes or a fashionable outfit. You need motivation. In fact, motivation is the key to all that follows. You have to motivate yourself to run on a nearly daily basis. Not now and then, but nearly daily.

Motivation is important for all runners, but particularly so for beginners who have not yet had a chance to recognize the positive values of running, values that are not always easy to explain or measure. Before you take your first steps, establish a goal. Do not give up until you reach that goal. Many people start exercising to lose weight. Some people exercise as a means to quit smoking. Others set goals of relieving stress or finding private time for themselves. Establishing mileage goals works for many. Whatever your goal, motivate yourself to reach it.

The following advice I am about to offer is important. In fact, very, very important: Start slowly. Very slowly. This might mean that your first running step could actually be a walking step.

You will have fewer problems with sore muscles or other injuries if you don't train too hard the first few days, or even the first few weeks, or even the first few months. Think of how long it took for you to get out of shape. Did it take 10 years, 20 years, 30 years, whatever? Getting back in shape will not happen overnight. And if you have never been in shape, have never exercised or participated in any athletic endeavor, it may require more patience on your part. That doesn't mean the journey toward your first half marathon will be difficult, it will just take time. As a matter of fact, the more time you take to prepare, the easier it will be. You will enjoy running much more if you try to do less than you're capable of accomplishing those first few days. You will also achieve more, because the most important factor in achieving success is consistency. Also, consider this fact: The slower you are, the easier it will be to improve. When you're down on the bottom, the only way is up.

Denise Daney, 37, a medical claims analyst from Lithia, Florida, remembers very clearly her first day of running. "I couldn't run longer than 30 seconds and I felt like I was going to die." As part of her motivation, Daney had signed up for a 5K race and wondered how she could possibly run that 3-mile distance without stopping. Yet within the next few years, she had run multiple 5Ks, a pair of 10Ks, and three half marathons. "I've learned never to question my abilities," she now says.

Among those who chose an easy beginning is Craig Daniels, 43, a teacher from St. Croix, Virgin Islands. After walking for two months, building up his distance, he finally decided to try running a bit. "I made about a half mile, but was elated with that accomplishment. I swore that the next day I would run just as far, and a bit farther if possible. Each day, I built upon my previous day's distance." Daniels says that all it takes to become a runner is perseverance and determination.

A friend's post on social media inspired Kristine K. Nass, 44, a teacher from Edwardsburg, Michigan. "A friend of mine had just completed her first half marathon and described it in a Facebook post." Nass says. "I messaged her that very minute and asked how do I begin? She told me to put one foot in front of the other and just go! I did what she suggested, and I am not going to lie: I was sore all the time, but less than six months later I finished my first half marathon with a time of 2:15. I cried when I crossed the finish." Nass has continued to run half marathons and even persuaded two nonrunner friends to join her. She says, "Running taught me not to fear beginnings."

A Sense of Accomplishment

Angela Russell, 36, a stay-at-home mom from Tacoma, Washington, first took a running class in college: "I needed the credits, and the sailing and fencing classes filled up. That class sparked an interest, and on a whim, I signed up for a 5K, the St Patrick's Day Dash in Seattle. I had no clue what I was doing. I pinned the bib to my back, instead of my front! But when the gun sounded, and I hit the streets of Seattle with thousands of people, I felt a swell of emotion. I still remember that, more than 15 years later. I didn't know why I was so emotional at the time, but in hindsight, I think it's because it was then I realized I discovered something that would have a huge impact on my life. Since then, I've finished many more 5Ks, about a half dozen 10Ks, five half marathons, and three full-distance marathons. Running has both humbled and inspired me like nothing else has. It has given me a deep sense of accomplishment and satisfaction, and I can't imagine not running now."

30/30 Plan

New runners come to the sport from all directions. Often it is because they decide to run a specific race, whether half marathon or not, or motivation may come from elsewhere. However, many who start have no directions.

Here's my dirty, little secret. You don't need me in order to start as a runner. Many people begin to run without having yet subscribed to *Runner's World*, without having read a training book, without doing a "how to run" search on the Internet. But as long as you have this book in hand, I might as well offer advice that just might make your start-up easier.

The best approach for beginners is to start by walking, then after you feel comfortable with that basic fitness exercise, begin to include jogging (easy running) in your routine. Jog, walk. Jog, walk. Jog, walk. Eventually you will be able to jog continuously, both farther and faster. How fast you progress depends on you, but do not be in a hurry to run fast or run far.

Here is a simple plan to get you going, featuring 30 minutes of exercise for the first 30 days. For that reason, I call it the 30/30 plan. It is a routine similar to one that the late Chuck Cornett, a coach from Orange Park, Florida, used with beginning runners. I first met Chuck at one of Coach Roy Benson's running camps in Asheville, North Carolina, and was most impressed with the simplicity of how he taught and inspired those new to our sport.

Here's how the 30/30 plan works.

1. Walk out the door and go 15 minutes in one direction, turn around, and return 15 minutes to where you started: 30 minutes total.

2. For the first 10 minutes of your workout, it is obligatory that you walk: No running!

3. For the last 5 minutes of your workout, it is obligatory that you walk: Again, no running!

4. During the middle 15 minutes of the workout, you are free to jog or run—as long as you do so easily and do not push yourself.

5. Here's how to run during those middle 15 minutes: Jog for 30 seconds, walk until you are recovered, jog 30 seconds again. Jog, walk. Jog, walk. Jog, walk.

6. Once you feel comfortable jogging and walking, adapt that 30/30 pattern: jogging 30 seconds, walking 30 seconds, and so on.

Follow this 30/30 pattern for 30 days. If you train continuously (every day), you can complete this stage in a month. If you train every other day, it will take you two months, a 30/60 plan. Do what your body allows. Everyone has a different ability to adapt to exercise. When you're beginning, it is better to do too little than too much.

Here is another important point: Practice consistency. Unless you are injured, never go two days without working out. Even if busy, try to do something that second day. And if you do miss that second day, try extra hard to run the third. Or the fourth. Fitness lost is difficult to regain. You can't make up for lost days. They are gone forever, and trying to catch up by adding miles to future planned workouts is the worst sort of training error. Consistent training can help you achieve success.

Continue this 30/30 routine for 30 days, or 30/60 for 60 days, and you will find yourself able to cover 1 to 2 miles (1.6-3.2 km) walking and jogging. You are now ready to progress to the next stage of your training as a beginning runner.

Do not expect every run to be perfect. In fact, one of the common complaints of beginners is that running is not the perfect experience that all the books and articles in fitness magazines suggested it might be. Part of the reason is that beginners may push themselves too hard at first—particularly if they start training for a marathon without much background. If you try to run hard or fast every day, no wonder running is a struggle. Start gently. Don't be afraid to walk. Keep the pace at a conversational level. Don't run too many miles too soon. A gradual beginning will allow you to have a satisfying end.

5 | Why We Run

Shelley Goss Hussman, 54, a paralegal from Visalia, California, did not start running seriously until 2008. Hussman once hated running, even though she always had been active in dance and aerobics. "But once I got past my 3-mile (4.8 km) 'wall,' I was surprised at how easy it became and how much I loved running," she says. She now has run two dozen half marathons and two fulls.

Yasia Zinko Sorbo, 39, a personal trainer from Staten Island, New York, enjoys the freedom and the ability to be in control. "I miss all that while I'm busy being a mom," explains Sorbo,

Amy Huerta, 48, a social worker from Alameda, California, revels in the opportunity to be alone. It allows her time to think. Huerta adds, "Running keeps me in shape. And I find the daily challenge incredibly rewarding. Every time I go out into the fresh air, the sun, and the wind, I come home happier and at peace."

Runners love to run. Make no mistake about it. While nonrunners sometimes mistakenly believe that we are mostly interested in physical fitness—and, yes, sometimes it is that—the main reason we run is because we love doing so. Sounds like too simplistic an explanation, but it's true. Running is fun. It's an expression of our bodies, our well-being. We like the feeling of the wind in our hair. But there are myriad reasons why we run, as I discovered recently when I posted a link on my Facebook page to a blog post on the subject.

The post, "10 Reasons Why I Run," was written by Ashley Weingart, who writes the blog *Running with Skissors*. The first reason, explains Ashley, is freedom: "No to-do list. Nothing. Just me, myself and the road."

Weingart's post (see 10 Reasons Why Ashley Runs) definitely resonated with readers after I posted a link to it on my Facebook page. Facebook allows me to measure the popularity of items I post. Within 48 hours, her 10 reasons achieved more than 100,000 "reaches," a thousand "shares" and several hundred comments from those who visit my page regularly.

Among the commenters, Brooke Guzma, 31, a municipal secretary from Clinton, Pennsylvania, claimed 2 reasons for why she ran, not 10. "The first reason I run is to be healthy and active," Guzma posted. "I want to get in shape, lose weight, and stay in shape. The second reason is more personal. I run to honor my father. He was a runner. He ran the New York City Marathon five times, also Boston, Marine Corps, and two 50-milers (80 km). One of my earliest memories was running around the local park with him. He is, and always will be, my inspiration. My dad was diagnosed with bone cancer in 2004. He beat it, but lost a lot of use in his left arm, which meant he could not run anymore. I had lost touch with running, but decided to get back into it in 2011. I ran my first half in 2012 and my first full in 2013. My dad was there both times to watch me complete something I only dreamt about. And I know he is very proud of me. My father and I are really close, and running made that bond even stronger."

People run to stay in shape, to feel part of a community, and sometimes just to reach the end, knowing that they have achieved their goals, a feeling that can be shared with other runners.

Marathonfoto.com

10 Reasons Why Ashley Runs

Ashley Weingart, who writes the blog *Running with Skissors*, admits that she used to hate running. "I despised it," Weingart writes. "The only time I ran was when I was forced to do so in gym class." After her third pregnancy, she started running to lose weight, and hate turned to love. Weingart offers these 10 reasons why she now loves to run:

1. **Freedom:** No purse with diapers, wipes, pacifiers, or snacks. No children asking for anything and everything. No to-do list. Nothing. Just me, myself, and the road. Running equals liberation.

2. **The great outdoors:** When I say I love running, I don't mean on a treadmill. My love affair is with the road, the trail, and all the landscapes that surround me. Getting outside for a run feeds my soul.

3. **Therapy:** When I'm running, I literally let it all go. I run to get rid of the crazy. I sweat it out, I breathe it out, I run it out. Seriously, it is free therapy. Better than wine.

4. **It's free:** No gym membership needed. No checks to write. No class times to work around. Just walk out the door. Then run.

5. **Races:** Training is the hard part. Racing is the reward. While I'm almost always nervous, the excitement at the start is energizing. The pride I feel when crossing a finish line is hard to describe.

6. **Great exercise:** It's no secret that running is a great exercise. You burn calories like mad, and it's a super cardio workout that has helped me get healthier than ever before.

7. **My own music:** While I usually turn off the tunes during trail runs so I can pay attention to the rocks and roots, my time running is when I get to jam to my favorite songs.

8. **Start and finish:** There are few things in life that have a start and a finish. The laundry, the dishes, picking up toys seem never ending. When I run, I know that I can check it off the list and say, "Check! Done!"

9. **Feel alive:** When I run long distances, a feeling comes over me impossible to put into words. Some call it a "runner's high." I push as hard as I can and feel every piece of my body. To me it is empowering.

10. **Self-doubt, self-love:** Before a run, especially a long one, I am always nervous. There is a lot of self-doubt. Then I go out and kill it. There is no better feeling than running through the self-doubt and achieving a goal.

Jessica Hastad Rolwes, 29, a manager from Des Moines, Iowa, another Facebook friend, also started running as a way to get in shape. It provided her with a quick and easy way to burn calories. "I keep running," she says, "as it has become my 'me time.' Running is therapeutic, and I solve a lot of problems while out on a long run."

"I run because I enjoy traveling to new places to run in half marathons," states Samantha McGlynn Librea, 36, a schoolteacher from Rota, Spain. "I also found that having a training plan makes me stick to my workout goals.

Mindy Parton Campbell, 38, a homemaker from Winchester, Kentucky, started running because of the Boston Marathon bombing. "My niece was there that day," she remembers. "I was home on crutches, recovering from hip surgery and terrified for her safety and the safety of her running friends. I made a vow to myself that I would run the Boston Marathon someday. Someday I will get there. In the meantime, I've run one half marathon, and I'm training to run my first full."

Kim Nickerson Koncsol, 44, a manager from York, Pennsylvania, started to run to stay fit and do a 5K with a group of people: "I keep doing it because of the running community and the awesome conversations with friends at 4:30 in the morning."

Staying in Shape

Stacey Saunders, 38, a stay-at-home mom from Irmo, South Carolina, started running in June 1999 because she faced something new and unwanted: a permanent off-season. "Out of college, I had nothing to train for anymore after more than eight years of team sports," she says. A coworker was training for the Chicago Marathon and Saunders joined him "just to stay in shape." Saunders adds, "I've been running ever since (in between pregnancies). I keep running because (1) it gives me a feeling that no other sport or exercise gives me, (2) I can, (3) races give me structure and focus in training, and (4) running is free."

Bridget Knepp, 38, a stay-at-home mom from Bettendorf, Iowa, says, "I run for myself. I run for my health. I run to get away from my surroundings. I hate to run. I love to run. I hate to run. I love to run. I run to show my kids how to exercise to stay healthy. Running is the cheapest way to exercise. I love to run road races and now that my 10-year-old has started beating me, I love to watch him run. To see him passing grown men and women makes me smile and makes me pick up my own pace. The feel of crossing the finish line is a sense of accomplishment like nothing else. It doesn't matter if I'm first, last, or somewhere in between. It just matters that I did it. Step out the front door and just go! That's my motto."

Am I Getting Fitter?

"The whole point of training," write Stephen J. McGregor, PhD, and Matt Fitzgerald in *The Runner's Edge: High-Tech Training for Peak Performance*, "is to increase your running fitness. More exactly, the point is to gradually increase your race-specific fitness until it reaches a peak level at the time of your most important race. So the one question you want to answer more than any other throughout the training process is this: Am I getting fitter?" (McGregor and Fitzgerald 2010, p. 93)

Sedentary people, those who perhaps unfortunately are referred to as couch potatoes, do not always understand why we run. Unless they have someone in their immediate family who is a runner, and sometimes even then, they do not comprehend why we hit the highways, in bad weather as well as good, and waste an hour or so of our time each day training. They dredge up the memory of Jim Fixx, the author of the best-selling *The Complete Book of Running*, who died at the end of a 10-mile (16 km) training run. I can't fault them. Runners sometimes arrogantly look at couch potatoes as beneath them. I don't agree with that point of view. I just know that we are going to keep running whether or not other people understand.

What other people might not understand may be that getting in shape does not have the priority in their lives as it has with those of us who run half marathons or hope to run half marathons. But there is more to the half marathon than running 13.1 miles on a single day. It is the training to run that distance that serves as the bulk of the iceberg unseen beneath the ocean's surface. The runners quoted in this chapter know it because they experienced it. Running is wonderful. But the half marathon remains the carrot dangled before our noses as we prepare to run 13.1 and attach the semi-obligatory sticker with that number to the back of our cars.

What does training for the half marathon do for us? It helps us to lose weight if we are overweight. It strengthens our muscles, some more than others, and makes us fitter individuals. It provides a sudden 90-degree turn away from what previously had been an unhealthy lifestyle. From observing my fellow runners over a long lifetime, I can tell others that, in general, runners do not smoke; runners do not drink; runners eat healthy; runners are the first to leave the party (because they have a long run the next morning); runners live longer because of their lifestyle; and finally, runners are generally good people. If runners share a single vice, it is that we know all this and sometimes babble incessantly about our marvelous experiences even though our friends may not want to know our mile splits.

Enjoying the Solitude

Typical of our breed is Skip Steiner, 67, a retired Episcopal priest from Lusby, Maryland, who posted to my Facebook page "I love to run. In the past I had some good running partners, but lately I run alone. I find now I enjoy the solitude, but during a race I often talk with anyone nearby. I think running is good for my health. I started running in high school in 1962, and continued my first two years of college. I have stopped and started many times, but I plan to run as long as I am able. I still want to qualify for Boston."

Kelli Kerkhoff, 41, a stay-at-home mom from Wilmington, North Carolina, adds, "Running is something that makes me truly happy and is my own. I think, I vent, I laugh, I cry when I run. I come back home happier, healthier, and refreshed—even after a hard speed session."

Jen Veigel, 38, a teacher from Canton, Ohio, started running to find a healthier version of herself. Veigel says, "I was obese and very unhappy. I started slowly losing weight and finding myself again. I was astonished that I was able to run a half marathon. I continue to run because it's my sanity. It's my 'me' time. It's where I spend my time with God and my thoughts. It's where I continue to prove myself wrong, and it's where I find my strength."

"Running is the only thing I do 100 percent for myself," states Anita Zuniga, 26, an analyst from Santa Barbara, California. "I ran hurdles in high school, and after I graduated, I ran occasionally for exercise. I started running seriously for a few reasons: My dad ran a half marathon, which made me feel wildly out of shape for a 20-year-old, I bet an ex-boyfriend I'd start running regularly if he'd kick his caffeine habit, and most important, running makes me feel healthy, self-confident, and strong." Zuniga has run five half marathons and looks forward to improving her performance and eventually running a full.

Michelle Durivou, 46, a dental hygienist from Florida, started running after spending her childhood and teen years as a gymnast. After retiring from that sport at the age of 15, Durivou discovered she could not sit still, so she joined the track team. "I was so short," she says, "but I did love to run, so I have been doing so off and on since then. The main reason is that I find running to be relaxing."

Tammy Grossberndt, 51, a high school registrar from Flanders, New Jersey, started running after her 23-year-old daughter asked if they could train for a 5K together. Grossberndt replied that she did not think herself capable of running or even walking that far: "I was 48 years old and obese. But as a way to do something with my daughter I agreed. The rest is history. Since then I have completed many races ranging from 5K to a full marathon. I've also completed a Half Ironman. I am currently training for my second marathon and another Half Iron. I now run because I love how strong I've become. I've lost 30 percent of my bodyweight. I run because it is my therapy. I run because it is my playtime."

Playing with her great nephews wore out Angie Rogers Nishnick after only an hour. Nishnick, 41, from Portsmouth, Virginia, realized how out of shape she had allowed herself to become. She started working out and lost 60 pounds (27 kg), going from 206 (93 kg) to 154 pounds (47 kg), but did not start running until after the first year. "After my first 5K, I fell in love with the feeling of accomplishment. Races helped me rebuild a lost self-esteem. They allow you to set a goal and accomplish it. I replaced self-doubt with determination. Running has helped me inside more than outside, although I won't complain about the outside results." Nishnick was preparing for her first half marathon when she posted those comments to my Facebook page.

After getting laid off from her job a half dozen years ago, Kelley Scott Spencer, 54, a behavioral specialist from Reading, Pennsylvania, discovered the firing to be a mixed blessing. Spencer had run cross country in high school, then found herself busy both working and raising five children. She finally ran her first marathon at age 50. "It was something I always had wanted to do, but I never before had the time or energy," she says.

Daniel Reed, 56, a truck driver from St. Joseph, Michigan, began to run when a personal trainer put him on a treadmill and told him to walk a 5K. "Once I could do that," says Reed, "I started running on the street. Eight half marathons and two marathons later, I can now call myself a runner," he says.

Stacy Saunders, 35, a clinical psychologist from Ironton, Ohio, prefers running with others. "I run for the camaraderie," says Saunders. "Running opened my eyes to a whole new type of connectivity with others. Not the forced, social event, itchy dress, squeaky shoes sort of friendship. But real, honest, 'Don't talk to me right now. I'm training.' And I love you, I hate you, sweat-and-tear-forged friendship. I have rarely found that anywhere else."

"For me, running creates a special bond," Saunders continues. "People who train together share a heartbeat, fear the same giants, pray the same prayers, and dream the same dreams. To know that sort of kinship is to allow yourself to be stripped down onstage in front of your peers so that they may build you back up, step by step, mile after mile. I believe that is why when runners get injured or run their last miles, the entire running community is saddened. We all deeply feel that terrible loss and are reminded of our individual voids, filled over the years with miles, pancakes, medals, Garmins, safety pins, and, most of all, training partners. For me, the real joy and meaning of the journey to running, or an event, is not found in the event itself. But rather, it is the strength of kinship forged by shared transformation alongside fellow runners that far exceeds any individual measure of success. And that is why I run."

Nikki Warholic Heflin, 32, a high school teacher from Indianapolis, remembers her two aunts running. "Even as a young child, I saw the happiness and peace running brought them, and I thought it was so cool," she says. "I ran my first 5K at the age of 12, and with that race and all the others over 20 years of running, I always feel proud no matter how well I do. My aunts and I continue to share our running stories and serve as cheerleaders for each other."

And so we run for reasons as different as the number of runners in even the biggest races. As I've already said, runners love to run, make no mistake about it. Various runners can come up with various reasons for running—all of them valid—but I am convinced that in addition to all of the reasons offered here, we run because we enjoy doing it. For me, certainly, it keeps coming back to feeling the wind in my hair. If I have a specific goal, such as running a half marathon, all the better. Let me continue to lead you to the starting line of a 13.1-mile race.

6 | Hard/Easy

The question was posted to one of my online forums: "Why do my short runs of only 2 or 3 miles (3.2 or 4.8 km) feel so hard, but my long runs of 6-plus (9.6 km) miles feel so easy? One workout is awful, the next is awesome. Even with positive thinking, I dread those short runs."

It seemed a curious question. While as runners, new and old, we should not expect every run to result in the sometimes elusive runner's high, why would short runs prove harder than longer runs, assuming they are done at nearly the same pace? This seemed to go against conventional wisdom. Short seemingly should equal easy and long, seemingly hard. Still, I have learned not to dismiss the legitimate concerns of runners, particularly those new to the sport.

Let's approach the problem logically. Say on three successive days, you run first 3 miles, then 6 miles, then 3 miles; it would make sense that the longer 6-mile run in the middle should feel harder than the shorter runs on each side. Well, not necessarily, because you can't isolate a single workout without placing it into the context of all the runs surrounding it, not merely for days, but maybe even for weeks and months. How we feel during today's workout depends on yesterday's workout, and both workouts dictate how smoothly we run tomorrow. This was the answer I eventually offered the runner in the "Weekly Q&A" blog column I write for TrainingPeaks. com. Mainly I told the runner not to dread those short runs. They are there for a purpose.

"Adequate recovery is the key to success," writes John Davis in *Modern Training and Physiology for Middle and Long-Distance Runners*. "Adaptation is the recovery response to a stress; without a recovery period, there is no improvement. Long and fast running causes damage to your body, and the recovery response to this is the source of improvement" (Davis 2013, p. 31).

Hard/Easy Program Patterns

Let me nod now to one of my mentors: the late and great University of Oregon coach, Bill Bowerman. It was Bowerman who popularized the hard/easy approach, not only for his fast college track athletes, but also for ordinary runners training at considerably slower paces. More on Bill later, but fast or slow, the same principles apply. Run hard one day and you will need to run easy the next day for recovery. Run easy another day and the rest will allow you to run hard the day after that. Hard/easy. Hard/easy. Hard/easy. Thus I follow the lead of this great coach. If you analyze most of my programs, you will quickly see that I usually prescribe a hard day followed by an easy day or, looking at it from a different perspective, an easy day followed by a hard day.

As an example, here is week 3 of my novice 2 half marathon training program, which not too coincidentally includes a 6-miler (9.6 km) as its long run on the weekend.

Week	Mon	Tue	Wed	Thu	Fri	Sat	Sun
3	Rest	3-mile run	4-mile run	3-mile run	Rest	6-mile run	60 min cross

Here is how I would analyze that week, identifying the workouts each day as hard, easy, or rest.

Week	Mon	Tue	Wed	Thu	Fri	Sat	Sun
3	Rest	Easy	Hard	Easy	Rest	Hard	Easy

Two hard workouts a week seems reasonable for a novice runner, and maybe two or three hard workouts for an intermediate runner. As for advanced runners, they're a breed apart. They would not be happy unless I let them hammer away three or four hard workouts a week. Of course, it is possible to turn what is designed as an easy 3-miler (4.8 km) into a hard workout if you run that relatively short distance at warp speed, faster than race pace. And you can stroll a 6-miler (9.6 km) at a slow pace with walking breaks and time off to sniff the flowers so that it becomes a very easy workout, particularly for experienced runners comfortable with that distance. Nothing wrong with that: We all approach structured workouts from different angles. But while I can attach labels to my daily workouts in my instructions, and different runners can interpret and manipulate those labels and instructions in different ways, a pattern of hard/easy is an effective way to train. The pattern is important whether you are a beginner without a single race T-shirt (poor baby) or an experienced runner with dozens of medals hanging from hooks in your closet, so much bling that the glare blinds you when you open the closet door.

Hard/easy is not a new concept. At the 1896 Olympic Games, a Belgian runner was entered in the 100 meters and the marathon. When reporters quizzed him as to how he could train for two such diverse events, he said, "I run a short distance at a fast pace one day, and a long distance at a slow pace the next day." Really, training is that simple. And while I applaud everybody for trying to analyze their training using performance charts, sometimes you simply need to get out and run. Get your heart rate up to 80 to 90 percent a couple of days a week, do a lot of running at 60 to 70 percent most of the rest of the week, and once a week throw in something in between. Training is not that complicated unless we make it complicated.

Consider the pattern of the training programs you will encounter throughout this book. The pattern varies slightly as runners move from novice to intermediate to advanced programs, but let's start with the first of those, novice 2, using week 3 as an example.

Monday in my novice programs is a day of rest after a hard weekend. Tuesday is an easy day, because the run (3 miles [4.8 km]) is short. Then comes Wednesday. (I often refer to Wednesday's workout as a "sorta-long" run.) At 4 miles (6.4 km), Wednesday's run is not that much longer than Tuesday's workout in week 3, but it will peak at 5 miles (8 km) before the program ends several months later. Thursday is an easy day because of the slightly shorter distance (3 miles again), but many runners, including the one who questioned me, may find the workout hard, because they are fatigued from Tuesday and Wednesday. That's what I mean when I say you cannot take a single workout out of context and ignore what came before and will come after. Three days of running in a row is not that easy, so Friday offers another day of rest leading into the long run (6 miles [9.6 km]) on Saturday. With that rest day, of course, the long run should feel easy. It should feel *awesome!* Yes, the runner questioning me did have a good point. Next, Sunday: Cross-training on Sunday is designed to allow the runner to recover from the long run by choosing an aerobic exercise (such as swimming, cycling, or even walking) that uses slightly different muscles. I would classify this as an easy workout and hope that not too many runners following my program get out on their thin-tired titanium bikes for two- and three-hour rides through the rolling countryside.

Speaking of the end-of-week long run, while 6 miles (9.6 km) may not be that long or that hard for experienced runners, by the time my novice 2 runners reach the penultimate week 11 of their 12-week half marathon program, I ask them to do a 12-mile (19 km) long run, just short of the 13.1

Running hard one day and running easy the next will guide you safely through your training to race day.

Marathonfoto.com

miles they will cover in the race. (Novice 1 runners peak with 10-mile [16 km] long runs.) In my 18-week programs for the full marathon, runners do a 20-miler (32 km) in peak week 15 leading into a three-week taper. Hard/easy, hard/easy, hard/easy. You'll find that pattern running all through my training programs and the training programs of other coaches.

In my "Weekly Q&A" blog, I offered this recommendation to the questioning runner: "The way to combat (your) problem is to make the short runs truly 'easy.' Start slowly, perhaps even walk, then gradually build to a comfortable pace. Back off that pace toward the end of the run. Walk a bit before climbing into your car. This also would be a good time to stretch. And while you are running, enjoy the scenery, knowing your next long run of 6 miles (9.6 km) or more is going to feel awesome because you rested in the day or days leading up to it." Magnet these words of advice to your refrigerator: "Any time we run hard, we need to rest easy."

The Hardest of Hard Workouts

"What was your hardest workout?" I asked that question on my Facebook page. In the spirit of hard/easy, I wanted to find out what workouts seemed likely to crush the spirit of runners—but instead made them stronger. Here are a few of the answers. *Warning:* Do not attempt any of these workouts without sufficient preparation.

Sydney Sorkin, Leawood, Kansas: At a high school track, I run one lap at a fast pace, one lap at a recovery pace, then up and down the stadium stairs twice. Then I repeat the cycle, continuing 30 to 50 minutes. Ever since starting this workout, all the hills I have encountered in races have been a breeze.

Heather Topmiller, Cincinnati, Ohio: Running 10 miles (16 km) alone and mentally hating each step. It was a true struggle to run each and every mile, but I did. Training for my second half, I hadn't ran that far in four years.

Ginger Herring, St. Petersburg, Florida: Living in Florida and signed up for a fall marathon meant I had to run 20-miles (32 km) in oppressive heat and humidity. It was the kind of heat that sucked out all the energy and enthusiasm and made you want to give up the dream. I kept telling myself, "What doesn't kill me, makes me stronger." Those exhausting long runs helped me finish the marathon in a Boston-qualifying time.

Natalie Pewitt, Franklin, Tennessee: Running 8 miles (13 km) on the *dreadmill*. Complete torture!

Nancy Hunter Hatfield, McCall, Idaho: Running downhill 4 miles (6.4 km) from the ski lodge to the highway, then turning around at the bottom and running back up: 1,000-feet (305 m) loss, then 1,000-feet gain. Not easy, but definitely makes you stronger!

Kathy Aucter-Morse, Lowville, New York: Last year as part of my long run, there was a monster hill early on. I swore I never would run that hill, walking up instead, until a running friend said we were going up. I said "sure" but crushed that hill. I had been so intimidated, but I realize now I'm much stronger than I think.

Nancy Lehr, Lawton, Oklahoma: It was my last long run before my second half. About a quarter mile in, I fell. Scraped my knee, shoulder, and wrist. After a mile (1.6 km), it started to rain, not drizzle but a downpour. After the turnaround I was running back into the wind. It was freezing. It felt like pellets hitting your face. I was wet, cold, hurting, and crying, but I never stopped. I finished that run and was very proud of myself.

Except sometimes Real Life interferes with Running Life. Allow me to divert your attention briefly to the question of juggling workouts. What happens when illness, injury, a business meeting, a babysitting crisis, even a week's vacation skiing in Colorado forces runners to at least temporarily scrap their precisely followed half marathon schedules, allowing days or more to pass without running, or without following exactly one of my schedules presented in this book? How do you regroup? How do you juggle workouts so that you do not lose fitness, so that you do not divert from your carefully prepared upward path leading to a PR in your next half marathon?

What happens when you are forced into a pattern of hard/hard or easy/easy instead of the more sensibly crafted hard/easy programs shown here? Will lightning strike? Is it, "Arrivederci, bling?"

No, because it is less important what you run on any one day or two days and more important what you do over the weeks and months of a 12-week training program. Relax, take an extra day off if forced to. Run that 10-mile (16 km) long run on a Wednesday instead of a Saturday when you're leaving on that ski trip. I frequently get questions from runners worried that changing one of my training programs even one day or two will cause a drop in fitness. Relax, I say. Minor modifications do not matter. But major modifications? That might matter. At some point if and when you have to lose too much time from your training—the flu can cause that, a plantar fascia injury can cause that—you may need to reassess your goals and postpone that record-busting race.

Bill Bowerman and the Hard/Easy Approach

Back to Bill Bowerman and why I consider his training theories so important to those of you who had not heard his name until you purchased this book.

Hard/easy comes right out of the Bill Bowerman songbook. In any list of the most influential coaches, not only in the United States but also in the world, Bowerman would rank right up near the top. Bowerman attended the University of Oregon as a football player, who also competed in track. After graduation, he coached football for a while, but within a few years changed focus to concentrate on track and field along with cross country. Arguably, Bowerman ranks among the best-ever track coaches in the world.

Okay, I'm biased, but during two dozen years at Oregon, Bowerman coached 31 Olympic athletes and 12 American-record holders and his teams won the NCAA title four times. He also served as head coach of the 1972 U.S. Olympic team. Among his champion athletes were Peter Mundle, Ken Reiser, Jim Grelle, Dyrol Burleson, Kenny Moore, and the legendary Pre (Steve Prefontaine). Bowerman also was one of the cofounders of Nike with Phil Knight, originally a half-miler on the Oregon track team. The genius Bill brought to the business was shoe design. He didn't start to design shoes to make money (although eventually he would become a millionaire doing just that). He simply was looking for better shoes for the runners on his teams. While experimenting with materials and designs, Bill created the iconic Waffle Trainer, the name coming from the pattern of the rubber sole, created with the waffle iron he borrowed from his wife.

While best known for his coaching runners at the front of the pack in track meets and road races, less known is the impact Bowerman had on the middle of the pack and the back of the pack (joggers, if that term doesn't offend you), runners who take two or three hours or more to finish half marathons, five to six hours or more to finish full marathons. In 1962, Bowerman took a 4 × 1500-meter relay team made up of Oregon athletes to New Zealand at the invitation of Arthur Lydiard, another coach of world-class trackmen. Arthur invited Bill to jog with him, and the Oregon coach was embarrassed to discover that he was woefully out of shape.

Bowerman continued jogging after he returned to Eugene, Oregon, and also started a program for beginning runners at the local YMCA, working with W.E. Harris, MD, a cardiologist. The Bowerman and Harris training group would attain some fame as the Eugene Housewives. Bowerman enjoyed coaching people who had never run in high school or college, but he learned from them, too. Bowerman collaborated with Harris to write a small booklet, *Jogging*. Expanded into a book for Grosset and Dunlap, it eventually would sell a million copies and serve as the forerunner for the other best-selling books that followed by Dr. Ken Cooper (*Aerobics*), Dr. George Sheehan (*Running & Being*), and Jim Fixx (*The Complete Book of Running*).

One summer while vacationing on the West Coast with my family, I stopped in Eugene to see Bill Bowerman. Call it a pilgrimage if you will. Earlier in the year, I had placed first American (fifth overall) in the Boston Marathon, but fell short of my goal to make the U.S Olympic team. School was out, the track season over, but Bowerman was working with an Oregon graduate, Bill Dellinger, preparing him to run 5,000 meters in the Olympic Trials later that summer. Dellinger had participated in the two previous Olympics, but had failed to medal.

Bowerman immediately recruited me to assist in a 3-mile (4.8 km) time trial planned for Dellinger, using me as a rabbit, along with Archie San Romani, Jr., another Oregon track athlete, who had placed second in the NCAA 1,500 meters earlier that summer. Archie paced Bill for the first lap, I the second, and we continued alternating. Bill finished in 13:39, a fast enough time to win most races in that era. Then we alternated running 220-yard and 110-yard sprints.

The next morning, Bill Dellinger's wife drove the two of us 10 miles (16 km) out of town and left us to run back to Eugene along a dirt road at an easy pace, about 7:00 per mile (4:20/km). We chatted most of the way.

And that is my point. In coaching Bill Dellinger, Bill Bowerman, perhaps intuitively, was following the hard/easy approach that still works today. I do not know what Bowerman had Dellinger do the day after that, because

I left town, but that workout could have been hard, or it could have been a second easy day, the next day even a third easy day before Bowerman had Dellinger run fearlessly hard again. Later that summer, Bill Dellinger not only made the U.S. Olympic team, but he also went on to win a bronze medal at the Olympic Games in Tokyo. At the trials, San Romani, Jr., placed fifth in the 1,500 meters, missing the team by two places. Retiring, Dellinger joined Bowerman as an assistant coach and later succeeded him as head coach of Oregon for 25 years. Dellinger's most famous athlete was Alberto Salazar, four-time winner of the New York City Marathon and now a successful coach of elite athletes.

Jack Daniels, PhD, Olympian, coach, scientist, and author, makes an important point when it comes to the hard/easy approach, particularly the necessity for well-programmed periods of rest, not merely a day, but days, even weeks or months. "Rest and recovery are a vital part of a training program, not an attempt to avoid training," he writes in *Daniels' Running Formula*. "There may actually be times when you will benefit more from rest than from going out for another run, and sometimes doing a less stressful workout will produce more benefits than will a harder session" (Daniels 2014, p. 16).

Maximum Rest

What is the maximum length of time you can rest without losing fitness, without wasting all the time spent building to a peak. Richard L. Brown, PhD, writing in *Fitness Running*, suggests maybe as long as three weeks. He cites the case of Shelly Steely preparing for the 1992 Olympic Trials:

> Three weeks before the trials, (Shelly) ran a very poor 3,000 meters in San Jose. She told me she felt she was a little tired. As her coach, I was not surprised at her race result because some of her training in the previous two weeks had been a little off. Most coaches and athletes facing that situation believe that the answer is to train harder. What I had Shelly do instead, and she bought into it, was to put her running shoes away and knit instead of train for the next 10 days. She set a personal best in the 3,000 finals in New Orleans and made the Olympic team (Brown 2015, p. 52).

Moreover, at the Olympic Games in Barcelona, Spain, Steely not only made the finals, she finished seventh! Would 10 days rest before a major running event benefit every athlete, fast or slow? That is a question impossible to answer. You probably need to overtrain and be on the verge of injury before that much rest would help. As George Sheehan, MD, liked to say, "We are each an experiment of one."

Bowerman. Daniels. Different coaches use different patterns and systems to train runners fast and slow. No single method is better than all others. As important as the numbers you will see in the charts for my training programs later in this book, many other coaches successfully fill in their charts with other numbers. Often the most important ingredient is the desire of the athlete to achieve success. Such a desire certainly motivated my questioner quoted at the start of this chapter to wonder why his short runs felt awful and his long runs felt awesome. It would be agreeable if all our runs could be categorized as awesome. But singular workouts are only part of what will make you a half-marathoner, given that a 12-week buildup to a race of that distance consists of 84 days and 84 workouts. Let's consider next how 84 workouts might fit together in a pattern of success.

7 | Immediate Achievement

The minute you step out the door wearing your first pair of running shoes, just purchased at the specialty store, your body begins to change. A dozen steps maybe. It happens. Triggers occur. Changes begin. You are about to become a runner, and the body knows it must adapt. "This happens almost instantly," I was told by Scott Trappe, PhD, director of the Human Performance Laboratory at Ball State University. Scott and I recently discussed the science of fitness and the changes that occur to the human body the moment runners—especially new runners—begin to train for an event such as the half marathon.

Scientists like Trappe cannot measure these changes easily. Poets, maybe, but not scientists. The changes are too subtle at first. Actually, you, the runner, may recognize the changes before the scientists. You will get out of breath, for one thing. Within those dozen steps, you may start huffing and puffing. It will take a few more steps before you start to sweat, before your muscles begin to ache, before you are aware that, new shoes or not, the pavement beneath your feet feels harder than when you walked on it from the front door to the mailbox and back yesterday. Nevertheless, change has begun, its blast-off signaled by mini-explosions in the muscles.

Anna Twitty, 46, a legal processing assistant from Ventura, California, remembers her first days as a runner: "I felt exhausted, hungry, sore just about everywhere. I needed to ice my knees." A year and a half later, Twitty boasts, "I'm much stronger now. No more aches and pains."

It happens. Miracles occur. Former sedentary people become athletes. The outward changes often are easier to recognize than inward changes, says Ball State's Trappe. As you begin to burn more calories than you consume, you may shed a few pounds. You also may lose a pound or two by temporarily dehydrating. Whether or not you lose pounds, you may lose inches around your waist as you substitute muscle for fat in certain areas of the body. One runner admitted to me that after embarking on a fitness routine that blended strength training and running, she actually *gained* 20 pounds (9kg)—but lost several dress sizes.

Certain changes surprise new runners. Suzanne Bright, 31, a tour guide from Haleiwa, Hawaii, was surprised how much her calves changed. "They got so huge! Now I don't think about it anymore, but when this first happened, I was in shock."

Strengthening calf muscles (or any of the other muscles used to propel you forward), should make you a faster runner. That is why despite all the emphasis on strength training and cross-training and other training, the one exercise that will make you a better runner is running itself.

There can be downsides. Given their new exercise routines, newbie runners sometimes experience extra fatigue, even exhaustion, signaling that they may need to sleep more or eat more and drink more fluids to maintain energy levels. Or the opposite, they may actually feel exhilarated because of the excitement that comes with doing something different and achieving a certain undefined level of success.

An Experiment of One

As the late Dr. George Sheehan once said, "We are each an experiment of one." George served as our sport's philosopher. In his columns in *Runner's World* magazine and in best-selling books, such as *Running and Being*, Dr. Sheehan defined our sport, suggesting that we all react differently when prescribed running as a cure to all that ails us. Don't expect to react similarly to doses of exercise as does your best friend with a dozen half marathons completed, or that fast guy who rushes past you on the jogging path sure to reach Mars faster than the next spacecraft. Embrace the difference from other runners, but particularly from those who do not run. George is somewhere up in the Cloud smiling down on me as I offer you those simple words of advice.

Many people start to run hoping to lose weight. Is there a danger that new runners, like the woman mentioned earlier, might actually gain weight as they build muscle? That seems counterproductive. More often new runners will begin to lose weight as they burn calories. Burn more calories than you consume, and weight should begin to peel off. But don't expect overnight miracles in the area of weight loss. Cutting calories also is not a good idea. Eliminate carbs from your daily diet, and you will have a difficult time finishing those long-getting-longer runs prescribed in my training programs. Do not—repeat, do *not*—embark on a fad diet at the same time you file your entry form for a half marathon.

"Your best bet," suggests Nancy Clark, RD, author of *Nancy Clark's Sports Nutrition Guidebook*, "is to meet with a registered dietitian who specializes in sports nutrition." That sounds like self-serving advice coming from someone who has RD behind her name, but it is absolutely true. I've referred runners to Nancy's book and website, *nancyclarkrd.com*, for years.

Narrowing your search, you can ask runners in your area to recommend a nutritionist who understands running and the demands it places on our energy-burning systems. Ask also at the local specialty running store. Contact the local running club. Place a note in a bottle and hurl it into the nearest body of water. All sorts of services are available for runners, new and old, if you know where and how to look. Sports, Cardiovascular, and Wellness Nutrition (SCAN) is the largest dietetic practice group with 7,000 members of the Academy of Nutrition and Dietetics. The organization's website is scandpg.org.

"Together," says Clark, "you can create a food plan that will help you lose weight and maintain energy, permitting you to enjoy training even as the miles mount." She adds that no amount of training can compensate for an inferior diet.

When people begin to exercise, whether running or any other activity, they react in different ways. Don't assume from what you read in this book (or anywhere else) that your shift from a sedentary to an active being will result in reactions identical to those of the thousands, perhaps hundreds of thousands, who have preceded you in the path to a half marathon. You are unique. You are that experiment of one.

What changes can you expect? Some of those changes are obvious, sore muscles, for instance. Some are not. But what changes? You might be surprised as we examine the list: lungs, heart, arteries, capillaries, muscles, veins, ligaments, tendons. All these body parts and their functions change the moment we start to run. Let's consider some of these changes and how they eventually will help you become a successful runner.

Lungs

The huffing and puffing, they are almost the first thing that any new runner notices. Within a few steps you will get out of breath. Your breathing becomes labored and may cause you to doubt whether you are capable of becoming a runner. A simple run to the end of the block becomes almost impossible.

Are you different, some sort of freak? Here's a surprise for newcomers unaccustomed to the strains of a new sport. Experienced runners often get out of breath too in those first few steps. *Really?* Yes, really! Often it is because we start running too fast too soon, because we have not warmed up, because we run early in the morning, still sleepy, and because we are in a rush to get on with the rest of the day, but we're not going to give up our early run. *Excuse me: I know I am obsessed with running, but just get out of my way.*

First Running Steps

Julie Sweeney, 53, a writing instructor from Cincinnati, remembers her first running steps: "The breathing. That's what was hard. My favorite part of growing into a runner is knowing that now I can relax my breathing. I like how my heartbeats changed too. My body feels in sync and less stressed. I tell friends who say they can't run that it takes about six months of gradually training the heart to slow down and your breathing to lengthen. Then the joy and energy kick in. There are days when running is hard, but there is never a day where I've run any distance and regretted it."

For the most part, experienced runners do not notice this out-of-breath feeling because it is familiar to them. The systems in the body are not in balance, but the runners have been there before and done that and know that a few hundred yards down the road, at the end of the block, once the muscles and joints have been properly warmed and maybe after stopping to stretch, running will become easier for them—and it will also become easier for you.

The good news is that the lungs will adapt. Let's listen to the coaches and the scientists, the people who can tell us how our bodies function. "The permeability of the membrane that separates the lung tissue from the circulatory system increases and improves," Coach Roy Benson of Amelia Island, Florida recently explained to me, "but the lungs' capacity does not necessarily change. Everybody thinks that your lungs get bigger and better. That's not entirely true. The intercostal muscles that expand and shrink the size of the chest cavity when you breathe improve in strength and endurance. These are the muscles between the ribs that move chest wall and assist in breathing. The same thing happens with the diaphragm."

The somewhat bad news, adds Benson, is that from the standpoint of performance, this improvement will have very little effect on your eventual ability to run faster. "This is because the lungs have so much extra capacity that relatively little change results in the lung's actual ability to push oxygen into the circulatory system. Very few lung functions improve. The most important adaption is the improved fitness of the muscles of the respiratory system." But you don't need major improvements in your breathing to continue as a runner. So don't worry about the lungs or that three weeks into your new training lifestyle you still get out of breath. That's the new normal, but it's also the old normal.

If there is an important change in lung function, it probably is more psychological than physical. You get used to being out of breath. Any discomfort or anxiety you might experience retreats from your consciousness as you continue to run longer and longer distances. And if you do pick up the pace, either while doing a long run on the roads or going up a hill or doing speed work on the track, you still will get out of breath as your muscles, greedy as they may be, cry out for more oxygen. Let's move further into the body. What happens to all that oxygen you inhaled during your first run around the block?

Heart

While the ability of the lungs to supply the cardiovascular system with more oxygen is limited, the ability of the heart to transport that oxygen as fuel to the muscles improves, in fact, improves greatly, and the change begins to occur almost from workout number 1.

"The heart is a muscle," explains Coach Benson, "and like any muscle of the body it strengthens with exercise." The effect on the heart is like shifting to a lower gear in a sports car or on a bicycle. "Exposed to exercise, the heart's pumping action improves, gets stronger." As this happens over a period of days and weeks, the resting heart rate drops. This is a sure sign of physical fitness. The resting heart rate of the average person is around 72 beats per minute. Well-conditioned athletes have hearts that beat much slower; the best of them much, *much* slower. And much more powerfully.

That was true of my heart. One time at a medical meeting in Omaha, Nebraska, I sat next to Kenneth H. Cooper, MD, author of the best-selling books on fitness and arguably one of the key founders when it came to laying the groundwork for the running boom that began in the 1960s and 1970s and continues to this day. At one point during the lecture, Ken nudged me and said that my pulse was 29, an extremely low number. I knew that to be true because of having been tested at various human performance laboratories, but how did Dr. Cooper know?

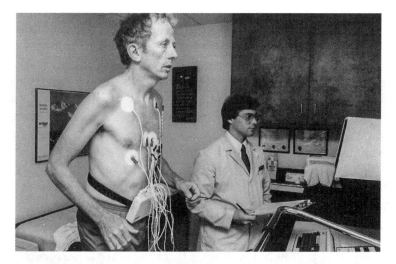

Hal Higdon, at age 60, taking a treadmill test at the Cooper Institute in Dallas, Texas.
From the author's private collection.

Never underestimate the curiosity of an exercise scientist. I had one leg crossed over the other. Ken pointed toward my ankle and a visibly pulsing vein. He had been able to count my heartbeat, but because of his study of athletes, both elite and back of the pack, my low pulse was no surprise to him. As for my maximum pulse rate, it would have been impossible to measure sitting in that conference room, but my max at that point in my career was 160. This was perhaps 20 or more beats per minute less than the predicted pulse rate for someone my age. It was a hint of my ability as a tightly trained endurance athlete.

Paul D. Thompson, MD, a cardiologist at Hartford Hospital in Connecticut, explained to me, "Your heart rate goes down very quickly, like within several weeks. This trained heart now is capable of ejecting more blood with each beat, pushing it from its chambers and into the arteries toward the muscles."

Luke Humphrey, who wrote *Hansons Half-Marathon Method: Run Your Best Half-Marathon the Hansons Way* with contributors Keith and Kevin Hanson, explains that the ventricle walls thicken, particularly the left ventricle. Thus, more blood can be pumped with less effort. And all this makes us better runners.

Arteries

Another exercise benefit, which has more impact on long-range health than on performance, is that the blood pressure drops "almost immediately, right after a single workout," says Dr. Thompson. This is a *major* benefit of running. It is a well-documented fact that if you can lower your blood pressure, you also can lower various cardiac risk factors.

Exercise improves the elasticity of the artery walls. Coach Benson suggests that with more elastic walls, blood flow may improve somewhat from the heart to the muscles. *Somewhat*, because he hedges his bet: he's not entirely sure that this health benefit will allow you to knock 10 minutes off your half marathon time. In this case, Benson suggests that runners need to think long term. Exercise and an improved lifestyle, including a healthy diet, will prevent or delay the buildup of artery-narrowing plaque, which otherwise could impede the flow of oxygen-rich blood to the muscles. This may not make you a faster runner at the age of 20 or 30 or 40, but it will make you a faster runner at 50 or 60 or 70 or beyond, because you will still be alive.

The effect on the arteries, thus, is preventive rather than active. "No evidence exists," write David E. Martin, PhD, and Peter N. Coe in *Training Distance Runners*, "that endurance training brings changes in arterial blood pressure that would contribute to an increased stroke volume" (Martin 1991, p. 78). In fact, suggest the coauthors, at maximum heart rate, arterial blood pressure is somewhat reduced. In other words, performance does not improve, but there is less danger of a medical emergency. Live to run. That certainly is my motto.

Capillaries

The big payday comes with the capillaries, the tiny blood vessels that permit oxygenated blood to flow from the arteries into the muscles and back out into the veins. Exercise causes what Coach Benson describes as "a huge expansion of the capillary bed," as much as a fivefold increase in the number of capillaries after a sedentary person starts exercising.

Capillaries are the minute vessels that connect the arterioles and venules. Their walls provide a semipermeable membrane for the interchange of substances between the blood and tissue fluid. That may be an overly technical definition for most of those who, like me, struggled through chemistry classes in high school and college. But think of capillaries as offering a revolving door into the muscles. They allow oxygen from the arteries in and, as the runner continues to run stride after stride, also permit the waste products to exit.

"Endurance training," says Martin and Coe, "brings a significant increase in the number of capillaries around (muscle) fibers. This decreases the diffusion distance for oxygen as it moves from capillary blood into the working muscle cells" (Martin 1991, p. 30). This is a huge plus for running as an exercise and for you as an athlete who runs. A huge plus!

Muscles

More than 600 muscles in your body work to create motion and force, and it is these muscles that permit us to run. Muscle tissue consists of long cells that contract when stimulated and produce motion—motion such as running, motion that propels us toward the finish line of a half marathon.

I once thought I understood how training strengthened the muscles. I thought I knew how, beginning with those first steps from the comfort of your living room into the frightening outdoors, you got stronger. Simple cause and effect, right? I'm less sure today exactly what happens deep down at the cellular level that permits you to become a better runner. When you initiate movement by sending a "move" signal from the brain to the muscles, it supposedly causes microscopic tears in those muscles. This has been described frequently as being similar to a paper cut to a finger. You inadvertently cut your finger on a sharp piece of paper. *Ouch!* The finger hurts, maybe even bleeds a bit, but you can still type at the computer. Eventually, the paper cut heals as do the microscopic muscle tears, and in healing, the muscle becomes stronger. Coaches sometimes referred to this as tear and repair. You tear down the muscles in order to repair them at a higher level.

That still is somewhat true, admits Ball State's Scott Trappe, but the explanation of how muscles strengthen is more subtle than that. Trappe explains that the scientific community has moved beyond tear and repair. Instead, Trappe talks about triggers and signals sent from the brain to the body telling it to shape up.

Trappe says, "We now have a much better idea of the molecular cues that occur during and after exercise and how these signals are involved with the muscle remodeling process. It's an integrative process from immediate signal activation to changes measured in minutes (epigenetics) to hours (genes) to days (protein synthesis). It's quite elegant."

Yes, those terms left me gasping, too, but consider the positive message: The minute you start to exercise, the benefits begin. No, you will not be able to run a half marathon after a single day's training, but the construction crew has arrived to build your house: the new you. That's an analogy used by Scott Trappe while explaining muscle building to his students, undergraduate and graduate, at Ball State University. It works for me, too.

Bricklayers

Consider that on day 1 of week 1, your first glorious day of training, workers arrive at the construction site, your body. The foreman has a copy of the building plans under his arm (my 12-week training program). He lays out the area where the new building will go, and the workers begin with a few bricks, then return the next day and lay a few bricks more, and a few more bricks on succeeding days. And at the end of the week, it should be possible to see at least the base of the new building. After 12 weeks, the building stands tall, and the workers throw their tools into the back of their pickup trucks and leave to begin work on another building.

Stretching the analogy to the human body, the rewards are instant. Each step taken your first day as a runner contributes to your physical fitness and your ability not merely to finish a half marathon, but to finish it comfortably, praising your coach as a genius. (No need to send flowers; a simple thank you posted to my Facebook page will do.)

The human body's bricklayers, adds Scott Trappe, do not take time off for lunch or head home for the night. On the weekends they continue their job. Scott's bricklayers never leave the work site. "As we continue to train, there is a good deal of muscle turnover, making muscle proteins to replace the used muscle proteins," he says. Thus body bricks benefit from continuous replacement—24 hours a day—as the training progresses. Even when you return to the couch, exhausted after a 3-mile run, sipping a sport drink and watching a *Fast and Furious* movie, bricks continue to be laid. The triggers continue. The muscles improve in speed and endurance. "This is true," says Trappe, "for both new runners and old runners."

As you continue to run, as brick is laid atop brick, you get fitter, and you get stronger. A 3-mile run that might have been a struggle during week 1 of your half marathon training, within a few weeks becomes easier. You may not necessarily be able to run that 3-miler any faster, but you become comfortable covering that distance. A half dozen or more weeks later, as you look back on that workout distance from the lofty pinnacle of 6 or 7

Moving in the Right Direction

Instant improvement: That's the guarantee. Once you make the decision to train for a half marathon, the moment you step out the door and start to run, your body will react by become fitter, by becoming faster, by being able to run farther, all the way to the finish line at 13.1 miles. In *Training Distance Runners*, coauthors David E. Martin, PhD, and Peter N. Coe, discuss how much you may improve.

"One of the most impressive increases is in the amount of oxygen, utilizable by the tissues," write Martin and Coe in *Training Distance Runners* (1991, p. 59). At rest, the body use 3.5 milliliters per kilogram of body weight per minute. This uptake can increase to more than twice as much as that possessed by untrained people. The breathing rate at rest for the untrained is 12 breaths per minute; a trained athlete may take as many as 45 to 50 breaths per minute while running. Total expired airflow, say the coauthors, can increase 40 times, from 6 to 180 liters per minute. Blood pumped out of the heart increases eightfold, from 5 liters per minute at rest to 40 liters per minute during maximum exercise.

Taking advantage of this powerhouse of energy are the muscles: "The working skeletal muscles may increase their blood-flow requirements from 20 percent of the output of the heart at rest to more than 85 percent during maximum exercise" (Martin 1991, p. 60). All this begins to happen the moment you decide to take your first running steps. You won't attain those high numbers on that first day, but you will be moving in the right direction.

or 8 or more miles covered in a single workout, you are going to think, "Why did 3 miles seem so long?"

That's the positive benefit of a well-designed training program aimed at the finish line of a half marathon, but here's the kicker in the Scott Trappe analogy. When Scott's bricklayers walk away from their completed structure, their work is done. The building will stand for tens and hundreds and maybe even thousands of years with only minor tuck pointing from time to time. Many consider the oldest manmade structure to be the Cairn of Barnenez. This stone monument in Brittany in northern France dating to 4850 BC is about as old as it gets. The remains of Shahr-e-Sukhteh, a mud-brick city in Iran, dates back to 3200 BC. The pyramids at Giza in Egypt were built in 2560 BC.

As humans, we don't quite last that long, thus after spending 12 weeks to build your structure so it will carry you 13.1 miles, you can't walk away from it like Scott Trappe's workmen and return 12 weeks later and expect to see it still standing. Minor tuck pointing may not be enough. To maintain your hard-earned muscle strength, you need to continue training.

This does not mean 10-mile (16 km) long runs as in the peak week of the novice 1 program, but regular doses of exercise, such as running or workouts in the gym or both. My main hope in telling you about Scott Trappe's bricklayers is that after your first half marathon, you will be motivated to make running a regular part of your lifestyle. "The more you run, the better you run," offers Trappe, as an incentive. How hard do you need to train to simply maintain, not build, your fitness? Without hard data to back this statement, I'm going to suggest somewhere between half to two-thirds your peak mileage leading up to a half marathon.

Meanwhile, back to the human body. The muscles absorb oxygen from the bloodstream. It is their fuel, similar to the fuel fed into an automobile. When an automobile burns fuel, the waste product of combustion is returned to the atmosphere as exhaust, not to be used again, a negative contribution to the carbon footprint besmirching Earth. When the human body uses oxygen-rich blood as its fuel, the oxygen-depleted blood is returned to the lungs and heart to be reenergized, an effective form of recycling.

The body achieves a pleasant level of stability, and with the blood flowing through the system, you can continue to run an increasing number of miles. But only with the activation and use of a few more body parts, beginning with the tendons and ligaments.

Along with the cartilage, the tendons and ligaments are the connectors that glue the muscles to the skeleton, your bones. Ligaments are fibrous tissues that connect bones to bones. Tendons connect muscles to bones. Training also will improve the strength of ligaments, tendons, and cartilage, but not as fast as it strengthens the muscles. The reason for this, suggests Coach Roy Benson, is because of a lesser blood supply to those parts of the body. "It takes weeks to begin to strengthen the tendons and ligaments," says Benson, "compared to the muscles, which become stronger almost overnight."

This poses a certain risk to the new runner, as well as to the old runner. Train too hard too soon, take less than the 12 weeks I recommend to prepare for a half marathon, and your risk of injury to the ligaments, tendons, cartilage, and bones increases. Unless you are biomechanically gifted like many of the runners born in Kenya's Rift Valley, you dramatically increase your risk of injury to these body parts. You can't get to the finish line of a half marathon unless you first get to the starting line. For many new runners, even the 12 weeks in one of my programs leading to a half may not be enough. Ideally, these nouveaux runners should prepare themselves for the demands of their training program. Lower the angle of the ramp leading upward, and it becomes easier to climb. I cannot guarantee that you will not get injured, but you definitely will lower your risk. The important thing is that you first put one foot and then the other on that ramp.

8 | Base Training

How do you encourage new runners? How do you convince them to take that first step out the door? It is not easy. But millions of people have taken that first step, otherwise we would not see the interest in half marathons that we do today. That first step is difficult, but the next few steps over the next few days and weeks can be even more difficult.

"I have people all the time tell me that they hate running," admits Sandy Graf of Hauser, Idaho. "I felt the same back when I had to run in gym class. But decades later I gave it a try, and it just clicked for me." Bruce Benson of Champaign, Illinois, claims he has a formula for turning nonrunners into runners: "I encourage folks to do 5K and 10K races to get started. When the bug hits them, I talk about halfs and fulls." Says Courtney J. Hagermann of Bel Air, Maryland, "I remind people that running does not have to be about distance or speed. I am slow, and it took a long time before I wanted to run farther than a 5K, but now I love getting outdoors."

Motivation is wherever you find it. Knowing another runner like Sandy or Bruce or Courtney, who once stood where you now stand, helps. But you hold motivation right in your own hands: this book. All the programs in this chapter and the several chapters to follow offer motivation. They offer you a beginning—and an end as well. Give me the next 12 weeks, and I will make you a runner.

For experienced runners, veterans, longtime members of the running community, those of you who have run races at distances from 5K to the marathon and beyond, slipping into one of my 12-week half marathon training programs presents no problems. Piece of cake. You don't

The best training for the sport of running is running.

need base training. The first week of the novice 1 program with only a dozen running miles plus a touch of cross-training probably offers less mileage than you currently do. But if you are new to running, being asked to run a 4-miler (6.4 km) in week 1 (gulp) may seem almost insurmountable and scare you away from what should be a reasonable end goal.

"If you've been running only sporadically and have to give your weekly routine an extreme makeover to start training, it's going to be tough to stick with it," warns Jennifer Van Allen, coauthor with Amby Burfoot, Bart Yasso, and Pamela Nisevich Bede of *The Runner's World Big Book of Marathon and Half-Marathon Training*. Van Allen suggests that new runners not fret, that they can still run a half marathon (and full marathon) in the near future. She says, "Pick a date one year away, and work your way up to it" (Van Allen, et al. 2012, p. 3).

That certainly is sound advice, what you would expect to hear from the experienced runner-editors at *Runner's World*, but I'm going to cut that timetable in half and offer you a base-training program lasting 12 weeks that, added to the 12 weeks of my half marathon programs, will get you ready in 24 weeks, half a year.

For those of you familiar with my training programs in books and on the Internet, this base-training program is brand new. I designed it as a new program for wannabe runners without much of a running background. Without *any* background. Without any background in other fitness activities. New runners who may have just finished the 30/30 program offered in chapter 4. New runners for whom jogging even a mile seems a struggle. New runners scared by the 4-miler (6.4 km) asked of them in week 1 of the novice 1 half. New runners without a time deadline, without a goal race pressuring them to train too hard too soon. If that sounds like you, base training offers a great introduction to the sport of long-distance running.

And while you may be a veteran runner, an experienced runner, someone with a lot of bling hanging from hooks in your closet, pay attention, too. I am about to talk about base training, the advantages of building a sound base before erecting a progressive program atop it. You knew that. Or you think you knew that, but maybe you didn't. The principles of base building are as important to you as they are for the newest newbie.

Why? The reasons why some runners should enter the sport, taking the conservative route through a base training program rather that going straight to one of the 12-week programs that lead directly to a half marathon may not be entirely obvious. Let me underline several points made in previous chapters, particularly for those of you coming to the sport with a low level of physical fitness and those of you who may never have run, or even considered running, before. Start slow. Start easy. Don't allow yourself to be pushed along through internal motivation or pulled along by well-meaning experienced runners. All of my training programs move from easy to hard, and if you are a new runner, a rookie, a newbie, you probably need to begin at easier-than-easy. The finish line of a half marathon looms as an exciting goal for so many runners, new and old, but before you can get to the finish line, you need to get to the starting line—uninjured and ready to run. You increase your chances of success if you stretch the period of preparation. While all my half marathon programs last 12 weeks, adding an extra 4 weeks, 8 weeks, or 12 weeks of base training will increase your chances of success.

First Steps

Before you take that first running step, before you embrace week 1 of my 12-week program, or a base building period before that, shouldn't you be adding other exercises? What about strength training? How about stretching, maybe even yoga? Aren't strengthening and stretching good ideas, designed by experts to prevent injury and allow us to run faster?

Well, yes, but not now. I train regularly in a gym, using a half dozen exercise machines to maintain, if not improve, my strength as part of a total-fitness routine. I usually favor relatively light weights and high repetitions as best for runners. Strength training is good for us, but if you have never pumped iron before, you do not want to start doing so at the same time you begin a base-training program. First, get through 12 weeks of run training, then decide if you want to add strength training to your weekly routine.

The same with stretching. Will learning to stretch help prevent injuries? Based on what the sport scientists tell me, the jury is out on that. Several popular books on stretching promote not dozens, but hundreds, of stretching exercises. Add to that yoga, a discipline that has many devotees. All to the good, but for at least the first four weeks, let's pass strength training and stretching by and concentrate on running.

Base training, like most of my other half marathon training programs, lasts 12 weeks. The difference is that I have broken these 12 weeks into three 4-week phases. Depending on your current level of fitness, you can begin with phase 1, or you can skip past the first 4 weeks and begin with phase 2, or even go all the way to phase 3 and use it as a test to see whether you are ready to move on to novice 1 half with its 4-miler (6.4 km) at the end of week 1. Let us begin with phase 1. Definitions of the terms used in the following chart are provided after the chart.

I Can Run Faster

Christine Leonard, 29, an occupational therapist from Cambridge, Massachusetts, started running as a teenager. "I always thought I would simply be someone who runs 9-minute pace (5:35/km)," says Leonard. "I didn't follow any specific training plan and finished dozens of 5Ks around 27:00." Then in a space of 18 months, Leonard knocked that 5K time down to 21:00, also finishing a 1:34:50 half marathon, much better than at her old 9-minute pace. She credits two changes in her approach to running.

Instead of merely going for a run, Leonard focused specifically on training, in the sense that each workout suddenly meant something and contributed to achieving a specific goal. Leonard says, "I picked a training program and stuck with it. I now run tempo runs, track workouts, or hill workouts each week. Also a long run." She supplements that with strength training and cross-training. "Regular sprints have done wonders in building power and speed," she says.

More important, Leonard changed her attitude: "Previously, the only reason I laced up my running shoes was in a vain attempt to pay penance for consuming a block of cheddar or to compensate for feelings of guilt over living like a sloth. The more I started to work at running, the better I got. And the better I got, the more fun it felt until suddenly I realized, 'I run fast. I feel great. I can run faster.' I won't lie: My love is partly rooted in vanity, but now I run to feel strong and fast and free. Believing running has no limits has allowed me to push through the limits I once set for myself."

BASE TRAINING: PHASE 1

Week	Mon	Tue	Wed	Thu	Fri	Sat	Sun
1	Rest	1-mile run/walk	1-mile run or cross	1-mile run/walk	Rest	20 min cross	1.25-mile run
2	Rest	1-mile run/walk	1-mile run or cross	1-mile run/walk	Rest	20 min cross	1.5-mile run
3	Rest	1-mile run/walk	1-mile run or cross	1-mile run/walk	Rest	20 min cross	1.75-mile run
4	Rest	1-mile run/walk	1-mile run or cross	1-mile run/walk	Rest	20 min cross	2-mile run

Note: To convert English distances to metric, use an online conversion website such as www.onlineconversion.com/length_common.

Rest

I shouldn't need to define rest, should I? Actually I do, because many new runners are so eager to start that they want to bust out the door on the first day of week 1 and start running. Don't do it, more for psychological than for physical reasons. Stay attached to your couch on Monday of week 1 and contemplate the running that will begin the next day. Mondays and Fridays are rest days in phase 1 of base training. In fact, those two days bracketing the weekend are rest or easy days in most of my programs. Reflecting on what you learned several chapters earlier, rest is an important part of any training program, the easy of hard/easy.

Run/Walk

This is a combination of running and walking, suggested for those midweek days (Tuesdays and Thursdays) when you want to do some running, but only some. Nothing in the rules suggests you have to run continuously, either in training or in an organized road race. Use your own judgment. Run until you begin to feel fatigued, then walk until recovered. Run. Walk. Run. Walk. Jeff Galloway, a 1972 Olympian, has had an impressive career coaching runners to run and walk precise increments: 1 minute running, 1 minute walking, for instance. Or for the most fit: 10 minutes running, 1 minute walking. These are called "Gallowalks," with the breakdown between running and walking dictated by the individual runner. I am less precise than Jeff when it comes to dictating the shift back and forth between running and walking, preferring to offer those following my programs the option to walk when the mood hits them. The choice is up to you, but it generally is a good idea to insert brief walking breaks early in your workouts rather than being forced to do so toward the end.

Cross

Cross designates cross-training days. That term can cover a lot of ground, but I only count aerobic activities as cross-training. Soccer and volleyball are great sports, but you raise your risk of injury if you engage in those activities while training for a half marathon. Straight-ahead sports, good; sideways sports, bad. Better would be swimming or cycling, and don't discount the benefits of a good hike the day before or after a long run. Add to that cross-country skiing or snowshoeing. But not yoga, and not strength training. That offends some devotees of those disciplines, but I'll tell you why as I continue to discuss cross-training in more detail throughout this book. Wednesday is an option day: run or cross. How long to cross train? About as long as if you had run the distance prescribed, 1 mile in this first phase of base training. Choose your own aerobic activity. Saturday is a day devoted entirely to cross-training: 20 minutes in phase 1, more in phases 2 and 3.

Run

When I suggest run as I do for Sundays, put one foot in front of the other and do just that. It sounds pretty simple, and it is. A 1.25-mile (2 km) run in week 1 may not seem long, but this is the equivalent of the weekend long runs I prescribe for my half and full marathon programs. Don't worry about how fast you run; just cover the distance—or approximately the distance suggested. Begin with that 1.25-mile run in week 1 and add a quarter mile (.4 km) each week, reaching 2 miles (3.2 km) in week 4. Ideally, you should be able to run at a pace that allows you to converse comfortably with a training partner. Run easy. Don't push too hard or too fast. Is taking walking breaks permitted? I get this question often, so let me repeat what I said a few paragraphs earlier. Yes, permission granted! I have very few rules when it comes to teaching beginning runners, although I would prefer that you do the Sunday runs more or less nonstop with only minimal breaks.

Make it through the first four weeks of phase 1, and you are ready to move to phase 2: four more weeks of gradually increased amounts of training.

BASE TRAINING: PHASE 2

Week	Mon	Tue	Wed	Thu	Fri	Sat	Sun
5	Rest	1.25-mile run/walk, strength	1.5-mile run or cross	1.25-mile run/walk, strength	Rest	25 min cross	2.25-mile run
6	Rest	1.5-mile run/walk, strength	1.5-mile run or cross	1.5-mile run/walk, strength	Rest	25 min cross	2.5-mile run
7	Rest	1.75-mile run/walk, strength	1.5-mile run or cross	1.75-mile run/walk, strength	Rest	25 min cross	2.75-mile run
8	Rest	2-mile run/walk, strength	1.5-mile run or cross	2-mile run/walk, strength	Rest	25 min cross	3-mile run

Note: To convert English distances to metric, use an online conversion website such as www.onlineconversion.com/length_common.

Rest

Do you need a day's rest after your weekend workouts? You may not feel that fatigued, but yes, you do. The most important day in any beginning running program (intermediate and advanced, too) continues to be the rest day. Rest days can be as vital as training days. They give your muscles time to recover so you can run again. Actually, your muscles will build in strength as you rest. Without recovery days, you will not improve.

Strength

Here's something new for phase 2. Earlier I suggested that you not worry about strength training, at least not for the first four weeks of base training. But now, consider adding strength training to your fitness routine, and the best days on which to do so are Tuesdays and Thursdays, immediately after your run. When my wife and I are in Florida during the winter, I often run on the beach then stop off at the gym before heading home. In Indiana during the summer, I pause at a gym toward the end of a morning bike ride. Yes, fitness can be fun. This is not usually part of a planned program. I combine running or biking with strength training, because I enjoy those activities. And it contributes to my fitness. Should you be a little cautious about adding strength training to your weekly routine? Yes, you should. So doing so now is an option that can be postponed until a later training phase.

The Ramp

While working on this book, I reviewed the writings of several dozen running gurus and fellow authors, among them Tim Noakes, David E. Martin, Kevin Hanson, Pete Pfitzinger, and Jack Daniels. Check the bibliography at the back of the book for references. Despite small differences in each author's approach to training, we agree on one item: The Ramp. At its simplest level, effective training involves gradually ramping your miles upward. You begin on a sunny Sunday at the end of week 1 with a 1.25-mile (2 km) run, and by week 12 you run 4 miles (6.4 km) and suddenly realize that, hey, I'm getting in shape. It's what my fellow gurus call progressive adaption. You don't need a PhD behind your name to figure out how it works. Add a little bit more to your training formula each week, week after week, and you will improve as a runner. Trust the ramp: It will get you to the finish line of a half marathon. The ramp continues its relentless drive upward as we shift from phase 2 to phase 3.

BASE TRAINING: PHASE 3

Week	Mon	Tue	Wed	Thu	Fri	Sat	Sun
9	Rest	2.25-mile run, strength	1.5-mile run or cross	2.25-mile run, strength	Rest	30 min cross	3.25-mile run
10	Rest	2.5-mile run, strength	1.5-mile run or cross	2.5-mile run, strength	Rest	30 min cross	3.5-mile run
11	Rest	2.75-mile run, strength	1.5-mile run or cross	2.75-mile run, strength	Rest	30 min cross	3. 75-mile run
12	Rest	3-mile run, strength	1.5-mile run or cross	3-mile run, strength	Rest	30 min cross	4-mile run

Note: To convert English distances to metric, use an online conversion website such as www.onlineconversion. com/length_common.

Run

At the end of 12 weeks of base training, you will arrive at the point where you should be able to run 3 to 4 miles (4.8-6.4 km) comfortably. The only difference, other than mileage, between the first two phases and phase 3 is that on Tuesdays and Thursdays I prescribe that you run instead of run/ walk. As you progress up the ramp to higher heights, you will find that the ability to shift seamlessly from running mode to walking mode and back to running mode is a useful tool. But it's also a hoot to be able to run those 3 to 4 miles without stopping. Thus, as you continue to train, it will be you rather than me who dictates how to best apply my programs.

Compare now the final week of base training with the first week of novice 1 half, which follows. They are almost identical. The entire purpose of this first base-training program is to ready you for the second program, a 12-week program aimed at a half marathon. You should be more than ready to start serious training on your way to pinning a 13.1 sticker on the back of your car.

Week	Mon	Tue	Wed	Thu	Fri	Sat	Sun
1	Rest	3-mile run	2-mile run or cross	3-mile run	Rest	30 min cross	4-mile run

In prescribing training programs, I consider them as guides. Feel free to make minor modifications to suit your work and family schedule. The progression of running workouts suggests adding a quarter mile (.4 km) to most runs each week. That's one lap on most outdoor tracks. If you train on the roads or on trails, various devices can help you measure and map your workouts. If you prefer not to go electronic, don't worry about it. Approximate the distance. You can even use time-based training. If you can cover a measured mile (1.6 km) in 8 minutes, go from 8 to 10 to 12 to 14 to 16 minutes, and you will have covered about 2 miles (3.2 km). *About* is a useful word. You need to be consistent in your training, but you do not need to measure your progress in hundredths of a mile.

Most important is *that* you run, not *how* you run. On the other hand, as long as you picked a training program, you might as well follow it as closely as possible. A lot of runners take great pride in following my programs exactly as they are written. And I have to admit, doing so is a tremendous confidence builder. I enjoy it when runners remove the printed training charts from their refrigerators and bring them to a race expo for me to autograph.

If you are an experienced runner—an oldie, rather than a newbie—the base-training program outlined earlier will be too easy for you. Perhaps you already have skipped ahead to the next chapter, but then you won't be reading these words, will you? Nevertheless, even though you may not need a buildup before starting one of my 12-week half marathon training programs, sometimes it is a good idea to choose that path, dropping in difficulty as a means of recharging your battery, a mental recharge often being more important than a physical recharge.

The journey of many miles begins with a single step. It is now time to train for the half marathon. Twelve weeks to glory!

9 | Picking a Program

Some people suddenly decide to run a half marathon, enter online, and begin training for it immediately, goal firmly planted in their mind. Others approach that goal more cautiously. Megan Goudschaal, an enrollment specialist from Gilbert, Arizona, lost 30 pounds (13.6 kg) with Weight Watchers before running entered her mind: "I had lots of friends in my Weight Watchers group who were runners and who would come to meetings with their race medals. I wanted to find out what the big deal was and see whether I could do a 5K."

Going online, Goudschaal discovered one of my training programs for that distance and quickly got hooked on the sense of accomplishment running gave her. She ratcheted her training up from 5K to 10K and only then did she eye the half marathon. She finished her first half, then ran three more, four in a single year. "Running truly has changed everything for me," says Goudschaal. "I'm 35 years old and in the best shape of my life."

After completing her first 5K without a specific training program, Susan Szalczynski, 46, an accountant from Chicago, signed up for a half marathon training group at her local YMCA. "I did so mainly to gain more experience, not necessarily to run the distance. When my coach (Tommie Estka) said I never would know whether I could run a half until I tried it, I filed my entry. We ran long runs based on time, not distance, spending one day a week at the track."

Fjola McCreary, 34, a stay-at-home mom from Vars, Ontario, sifted through Internet articles and decided to design her own schedule based on the information she found. McCreary describes her program: "Four runs a week, long runs on Sundays, two 10-milers (16 km) before my first half." Most coaches would consider that a more than reasonable route to success. But McCreary admits to being injured half the time: "I was running full out for all my runs." For her next race (and all since), she modeled her training on the charts she found on my website. Most important, she followed the directions and tips I offered, one of the most important being "Do some of your workouts at a very easy pace." Success followed.

Search Your Way to Fitness

Where do runners go to find help? Many come to me. Search for half marathon training on the Internet, and you probably will arrive at my website. I conducted an Internet search while writing this chapter and, other than a handful of paid links (humility aside), halhigdon.com dominated the screen. They were the top three, right ahead of *Runner's World*. The three most popular links leading to my training programs were to novice 1 half marathon, intermediate half marathon, and half marathon training programs. (That last search result provides a link to halhigdon.com rather than to a specific program.)

A site rises to the top of the Internet search rankings for one reason, and it has nothing to do with advertising dollars. It is because people use a site. One way or another they find you. Internet search engines diplomatically recognize this fact, and make it easy for searchers who follow.

Club Coaching

Nicky Gautier, 39, a research associate in Shreveport, Louisiana, sought support after she decided to run a half marathon. Then living in Virginia, she joined the Charlottesville Track Club so she could participate in its half and full marathon training program: "The club had a coach, Mark Lorenzoni, who wrote us individualized programs specific to our current level of fitness, race of interest, and race goals. Mark also sent class participants weekly e-mails with tips and maps of the workouts planned for the weekend."

Those weekend runs also included aid stations featuring sport drinks and energy bars, all handed to the runners by smiling volunteers. The price of the class was $32 ($45 for nonmembers). A pretty good price, if you ask me. The program started in May and aimed at fall and winter races. Gautier trained for the Richmond Half Marathon. "I had just finished the club's 10-mile (16 km) training program with the same coach," says Gautier. "Before starting, I was overweight and out of shape and had never run before. I never would have been able to stick with it and be the distance runner I am now if it hadn't been for the club and all of the great friends I met through the programs."

But I am not alone in offering training programs for the popular half marathon distance, and while I am proud of my three-on-top status, the rankings can change from day to day. Runners seeking guidance can follow links into the *Runner's World* website or to sites offered by individual coaches and by running organizations such as active.com or competitor. com. Brad Boughman, author of the book *Half Marathon Rookie: How to Train for a Half Marathon and Have Fun Doing It*, also will guide you to the starting line. Jeff Galloway scores well. There seems to be no limit to the amount of free advice and paid advice you can find if you go searching. On the other hand, because you have my book in front of you, listen first to what I have to say.

No Excuse

Given the easy availability of sound training programs online and in books and magazine articles, there is almost no excuse for not finding and following a half marathon training program. It will make your march to the finish line much easier. Nevertheless, not all runners follow the well-trod path.

For her first half marathon, January Turner, 38, a judge advocate in the U.S. Army, stationed in Killeen, Texas, ran without a plan, without much thought to what distance she was covering every day. "I was in the military and took the attitude that I could accomplish anything. That attitude came back to bite me at mile 11." Turner struggled through the remaining 2 miles (3.2 km), but finished proud that she had run the entire distance. Moving on to a full marathon, Turner chose a training program to ensure the last few miles would not seem so difficult.

After buying a $30 pair of shoes, Vic Barthelemy, 60, a retired grocery store manager from Murfreesboro, Tennessee, began without a plan: "I just ran until I hurt. That got me about a half mile at first. Then I walked back. Worked up to about 7 miles (11.2 km) before the half. No consistency. No idea about rest days. Finished the half with a lot of walking, but suffered a stress fracture and had to take about eight weeks off. I enjoyed the running and the race atmosphere, so I looked at a lot of plans on the Internet and in magazines. Bought your book and used your plan for running. Best thing I ever did. Last month I qualified for Boston."

Beth Carlson was always very active in tennis. A horseback instructor, age 54, living in Rockford, Illinois, she says, "I decided to run a half marathon on a whim and just started running with no plan. I simply increased my distance with each run. Surprise, surprise: I injured my knee and never made it to the starting line. When I turned 50, I put the half marathon back on my bucket list. I trained using your novice training program and ran my first half without injury. I'm now hooked on running."

Start Short and Finish Long

None of the previous three runners were wrong in training as they did without guidance. They logically started at a short distance, and gradually, day after day, week after week, they covered increasingly longer distances. At the simplest level, that is how all of my training programs and the programs of other coaches work: Start short and finish long. But my training programs follow a pattern—and so do the training programs of all good coaches—that not only makes each daily workout easier, but also almost guarantees that runners will make it to the starting line, which is an obvious necessity if your goal also is to make it to the finish line.

If any of the those three runners made what is often impolitely labeled as a training error, it was to train too hard, to train too fast, to buy into the theory of no pain, no gain, which you sometimes see on T-shirts worn by high school cross country runners. As part of accepting that mantra, new runners also fail to recognize the importance of rest; they fail to take days off. It is

Developing a training plan and sticking to it will help get you to the starting line. Your training plan will also prepare you for the race so that you can meet your final goal: to make it to the finish line.

Marathonfoto.com

only when a runner rests that stressed muscles have time to recover and regenerate. Rest, I might add, does not always mean that you take the day off from exercise entirely. Maybe you run fewer miles than you did the day before. Maybe you run them at a slower pace. This brings us back to Coach Bill Bowerman's theory of hard/easy. I keep hammering on this approach, but hard/easy is the most important word combination in this book.

It is more important than strength training, more important than stretching, more important than cross-training. All three are promoted by various running gurus in print and online to immunize runners from injury. Can this be true? I say a qualified maybe, in fact, a very qualified maybe. Specific exercises can strengthen muscles. Specific stretching exercises (static and dynamic) can lengthen muscles. Specific cross-training can improve your aerobic capacity on days when the muscles you use for running need a day off. But taken in doses that are too large, all of these activities can cause injury rather than prevent it. You need to know what you're doing, and maybe you can't accumulate that knowledge without the support of a good personal trainer or running coach.

But rest? Everybody knows how to rest, don't they? Not necessarily, because some people don't know the meaning of the word. Does it mean slow down, or do less, or switch to a complementary sport? They don't want to take a day off. The Interdenominational Work Ethic affects us all.

Admittedly, rest can be relative. For a beginning runner, rest might be an entire day off. My novice programs feature rest days on Mondays and Fridays. My advanced programs feature only a single day of rest, usually on Fridays, but sometimes on Saturday before a Sunday race. I also often allow advanced runners the option to run or rest. For an elite African runner, a rest day might feature an easy 10-miler (16 km) in the morning and another run of 5 miles (8 km) in the afternoon.

Yes, I know: That's not you. Ignoring for a moment the fact that none of you reading this book have the incredible ability to finish a half marathon in a time faster than 60 minutes (the world record as of this writing being 58:23 by Zersenay Tadese of Eritrea for men and 1:05:09 by Florence Kiplagat of Kenya for women). Regardless of your potential or current time for various running distances, what patterns prevail not only in my programs but in the programs of most coaches? How do you get from point A to point B? Point A being your first week of training; point B being the final week of hard training before you step to the starting line of the half marathon itself.

"Let's start at the very beginning," sang Julie Andrews in *The Sound of Music*, "a very good place to start." Consider the first week of my novice 1 half marathon program. This is one of the easiest programs of any I offer online. The program assumes that the person following it has little or no background as a runner. Maybe that person spent a month or two training for a 5K or other short race or used the base training program in the previous chapter, before signing up for a half marathon, but maybe that person started week 1 as a total running rookie.

Is that wise? I'm not going to sit in judgment. We all have to start somewhere, and here is week 1 of the novice 1 half marathon program:

Week	Mon	Tue	Wed	Thu	Fri	Sat	Sun
1	Rest	3-mile run	2-mile run or cross	3-mile run	Rest	30 min cross	4-mile run

And here is week 11, the penultimate week of novice 1 half marathon. This is the toughest week of the program. For one thing, it requires the most distance run in a single workout on the Sunday with one week to go. After that, runners get a bit of a break. Week 12, immediately before the race, features a cut in mileage, what is known as a taper. Runners taper so that they are well rested on their day of glory. Yep, that means hard/easy again.

Week	Mon	Tue	Wed	Thu	Fri	Sat	Sun
11	Rest	5-mile run	3-mile run or cross	5-mile run	Rest	60 min cross	10-mile run

The progression from A to B is obvious. Monday and Friday remain the same, reserved for rest, but the runs on Tuesdays and Thursdays show a slight bump from 3 miles (4.8 km) in week 1 to 5 miles (8 km) in week 11. Mileage on Wednesday also shows an upward slant, from 2 miles (3.2 km) to 3 miles, but with the option to cross-train on this day rather than run. Cross-training on Saturday doubles from 30 minutes to 60 minutes. The biggest difference between week 1 and week 11, however, is in the Sunday long run: 4 miles (6.4 km) increases to 10 miles (16 km). That last long run might have seemed somewhat scary to someone looking at the novice 1 training program for the first time. After nearly three months of training, however, running 10 miles may not be easy, but it certainly is doable and prepares the new runner to make the jump to the 13.1 miles of the half marathon race.

A quick aside: Why do I prescribe only 10 miles as the longest run? Why not run 13 miles for a psychological boost to prove that you can do it? Answer: You don't need that proof. In all my marathon training programs, the longest long run is 20 miles (32 km) leading to a 26-mile, 385-yard race. For the time being, let me simply say, Trust me! Follow the full program, progressing a mile (1.6 km) upward each week, and you will not need that boost. We'll discuss this jump later in the book, and I'll also provide an explanation of exactly what cross-training I want you to do.

Moving on to novice 2, the progression is similar to that in novice 1. Here is week 1:

Week	Mon	Tue	Wed	Thu	Fri	Sat	Sun
1	Rest	3-mile run	3-mile run	3-mile run	Rest	4-mile run	60 min cross

And here is week 11. My two novice programs are similar in weekly miles, but slightly different in pattern. One difference is that in novice 1, the long run is on Sunday; in novice 2, the long run on Saturday. Can you flip-flop days from Saturday to Sunday, regardless of the program? Yes, you can, and you also can change workouts from day to day depending on your family and work schedule, but sticking as close to my program as possible continues to make sense.

Week	Mon	Tue	Wed	Thu	Fri	Sat	Sun
11	Rest	3-mile run	5-mile run	3-mile run	Rest	12-mile run	60 min cross

Continuing to analyze the mileage progression in my half marathon programs, let us consider intermediate 1, only a slight move upward from novice 2, at least if you consider total mileage. Here's week 1 in intermediate 1:

Week	Mon	Tue	Wed	Thu	Fri	Sat	Sun
1	30 min cross	3-mile run	4-mile run	3-mile run	Rest	3-mile run	4-mile run

This plan includes an extra mile here, an extra mile there. The major change comes in moving cross-training from the weekend to Mondays. This allows two runs (instead of one) on the weekends. And some of those are pace runs, where you run the same pace you hope to run in the half marathon. I want you to become used to that precise pace, and I'll have more to say in a few more chapters when I discuss my intermediate programs in further detail.

Here is the peak, week 11, in intermediate 1. Compare it to week 1, and you can see that the changes are subtle, but also important.

Week	Mon	Tue	Wed	Thu	Fri	Sat	Sun
11	60 min cross	5-mile run	6-mile run	4-mile run	Rest	3-mile pace	12-mile run

Intermediate 2, quite obviously, offers another step upward from intermediate 1. Looking for the differences (other than mileage) between the two programs? Take a look at what I have planned in the way of speed work.

Yes, speed work, a word that frightens many runners because it signals a major break between the programs done before and the programs undertaken after speed work is introduced. You don't need to take the large step between intermediate 1 and 2, but at least be aware of the change, which will be discussed more later. Here is week 1 of intermediate 2:

Week	Mon	Tue	Wed	Thu	Fri	Sat	Sun
1	30 min cross	3-mile run	5 × 400 m at 5K pace	3-mile run	Rest	3-mile run	5-mile run

And here is week 11. Look again at Wednesday: Ten 400-meter repeats, probably executed on a running track, although you can do this workout on the roads. That's far from being easy, but did I tell you that intermediate 2 was easy?

Week	Mon	Tue	Wed	Thu	Fri	Sat	Sun
11	60 min cross	5-mile run	10 × 400 m at 5K pace	3-mile run	Rest	3-mile pace	12 miles

Intermediate 2 is easier than advanced, and I have developed only one advanced program for the half marathon, unlike the two advanced programs I offer for full marathon training. Advanced half features speed work on two days: Tuesdays and Thursdays. Ignore for a moment the meaning of 6 × hill and tempo, as well as 3/1. All will be made clear in chapters to come. Here is the week 1:

Week	Mon	Tue	Wed	Thu	Fri	Sat	Sun
1	3-mile run	6 × hill	3-mile run	40 min tempo	Rest	3-mile run	1:30 run (3/1)

And here is week 11:

Week	Mon	Tue	Wed	Thu	Fri	Sat	Sun
11	3-mile run	6 × 800 m at 10K pace	3-mile run	60 min tempo	Rest	3-mile pace	2:00 run

The one thing that all these half marathon programs have in common is a steady progression in mileage and difficulty. That is the key to all my half marathon training programs. That will be the key to your success in training for the popular 13.1-mile distance, whether following a novice, intermediate, or advanced program. The choice is up to you.

One final comment: Be conservative in your choice. Often runners will question me: "Should I choose novice 1 or novice 2?" My kneejerk reaction is to guide them to the easier program. If you have to ask, you probably are uncertain whether you can handle the tougher program. That being the case, why set yourself up for failure? Pick the route that is most likely to get you to the finish line with the least amount of stress. If your first half marathon following novice 1 is a success, you will have ample time in the years following to ratchet yourself up to increasingly more challenging programs from novice 1 to novice 2 to intermediate 1 to intermediate 2 and maybe even to advanced. Enjoy the journey.

10 | Novice Training

When Caroline Bedard-Nower, 48, a senior project manager from Wethersfield, Connecticut, decided she wanted to run a half marathon, she contacted me online, posting a comment to one of my Facebook pages. Over a period of six years, Bedard-Nower lost 115 pounds, some of it by exercising, but without any major running goals in mind.

Now she had a chosen goal: a half marathon she wanted to run in September, partly as confirmation of her fitness. This was in February, meaning Bedard-Nower had eight months to train for the race. I liked her long-range thinking. Yes, my half marathon training months last 12 weeks (or three months). That certainly offers ample time for most people to gear up for a half. The extra five months leading to Bedard-Nower's chosen half would allow her even more time to prepare. When you consider that she had spent the previous six years gradually losing weight, Bedard-Nower definitely deserved a start on the printout of the training program attached to her refrigerator. Good thinking, Caroline! Haven't I already said in this book that the more time you have to plan for a goal, the more successful you will be in achieving that goal?

Bedard-Nower wrote "Good evening, Mr. Higdon. I have been running for four years, but this year I'm ready to start training for my first half marathon. I have not run consistently due to illness (Lyme disease), and I'm just getting back into it. I was thinking of following one of your short-distance (8-week) programs starting this spring, then transitioning to a half marathon (12-week) program at the end of summer. In the meantime, I will start cardio-walking and running short distances. What are your thoughts and suggestions? Thank you very much for your help and motivation."

Something in Bedard-Nower's plea grabbed me. Maybe it was because she was thinking so far ahead. Well, she's a project manager, so obviously she knows how to manage projects, the half marathon certainly qualifying as a project. Rather than offer a quick response, I promised to get back to her later when I had time to reflect on her situation. After all, "what are your thoughts and suggestions" is a pretty broad question that resists too brief a response. (In many ways this book is my response.)

A day later, I reached out to her: "Hi, Caroline. Sorry for the delay. It sounds to me like you are acting intelligently, taking time to ramp up the mileage leading to your first half. That being the case, continue what you are doing, namely the cardio stuff. I also see from your Facebook page that you are following CrossFit. Stay on course, and maybe this spring and summer, you can program a few races at short distances before it is time to switch over to half marathon training. As long as you keep the ramp slanting gradually upward, you should achieve your goal."

Bedard-Nower responded, "Thank you very much for your insight, Mr. Higdon. Yes, you are right, I recently started CrossFit training. I needed to boost my cross-training and thought this would be a good fit, allowing me to build stamina for long runs. Following your suggestions, I will start my Hal Higdon training in May, planning a 5K race in June, a 10K race in July, another 5K race in August, and finally my first half marathon in September: Rock 'n' Roll Montreal. Thank you very much for taking the time to provide your suggestions. I value your knowledge and experience. I will continue to read your Facebook posts."

On reading this response, I chuckled. Bedard-Nower pretty much had it figured out. She needed my help less than she thought. Obviously, she had one of my half marathon training programs, downloaded from the Internet, sitting in front of her on the desk or stuck to the refrigerator. What I had provided more than anything else was motivation along with an imprimatur designating that she was moving in the right direction. Later, in checking Bedard-Nower's Facebook page, I saw that after our brief dialogue, she had posted my picture along with the comment "Getting a message with wonderful suggestions from Hal Higdon on my half marathon training made my day and motivated me to continue on this fitness journey."

Motivation Is the Key

Motivation! That's the key word. That's what I'm selling. Yes, this chapter contains the novice training programs that will help you on your journey, the same journey Caroline Bedard-Nower was taking, but really, it's all about motivation, isn't it? If I or you or we can motivate someone to use one of my programs to train for a goal race, we may have created a runner

Crossing the finish line can be the motivation a person needs to get up and running.
Marathonfoto.com

for life. Having said that, let's talk about two of my most popular half marathon programs: novice 1 and novice 2.

When I first began to design half marathon training programs in articles for *Runner's World* magazine as well as on the Internet, I began with programs for three levels: novice, intermediate, and advanced. Seemed logical. The labels attached to those programs defined them. Novice was aimed at first-time half marathoners. New runners. Newbies. The new N-word. People with a gleam in their eye but very little background as a runner or as an athlete in any sport. My initial novice program was simple, easy to use, almost too basic, aimed at people only a few steps from the couch. If you could manage to cover 4 miles (6.4 km) in your week 1 long run, even walking part of the distance, you should be able to race 13.1 miles in week 12, the program's final week. Time after time after time—thousands of times—this was proved true.

The intermediate program offered more mileage, but also a day of speed work each week. The advanced program featured still more mileage and another day of speed work (two speed days a week). Only a small percentage of runners (probably fewer than 10 percent) could handle an advanced program without self-destructing, but it was important to me as a coach to have an upper-level program to offer this group.

Then as running became more popular, I became aware of a fourth group that was not being served. This growing fourth group consisted of runners who, after doing a single half marathon, wanted to run a second or a third or a fourth or a tenth half marathon with maybe a few full marathons thrown in between. By now, those in this fourth group loved running and prospered under my training advice. But my original novice program was just too easy for them, way too easy for them, almost an insult to their new-found ability to go for long runs with their friends on weekends whether training for a specific race or not. And the intermediate program did not match their needs either. It was not necessarily too difficult, but the extra mileage absorbed more time than they could chip out of their busy lives. Plus not everybody enjoys speed work, not even a single day of it.

Recognizing this need, I created novice 2 as a bridge between the initial novice and intermediate programs. This was a program aimed at runners who already were veterans of the road racing scene, who had paid their dues participating in at least a handful of 5K and 10K and half marathon races—maybe even a full distance marathon. They didn't want to back all the way down to novice, but they didn't want or need the extra commitment demanded by my intermediate programs. For that reason, I split my original novice program into novice 1 and novice 2. The differences between these two popular programs are small, but important. Let's consider the two novice programs.

To Plan or Not to Plan

Not every runner starts with a plan. Some runners simply start to run and work their training out as they go along. This is not necessarily advised, as you can see from the comments that follow. To spare these runners from embarrassment (and perhaps allow me to avoid a lawsuit), I offer only their first names.

"For my first half marathon," remembers Richard, "I didn't use a plan. Just ran three days a week and did long runs on the weekends." Well, even that was somewhat of a plan, but Annette fell somewhat short of even that level of organization: "I just went out and ran, increasing mileage as I was able. Bad plan. Got injured. Had no idea what I was doing."

Ellen seems to have had more luck: "For my first half marathon I joined a training group at the local Fleet Feet running store, which gave me a plan and a group to train with as well as coaches."

"I didn't use a plan," says Louise. "I just built up the mileage week by week, then entered a race. Looking back I'm probably lucky I didn't injure myself."

I'm not going to argue with Darci's approach: "I found a few plans online, but basically created my own based on what those plans suggested. I had to do what worked for me and my crazy schedule."

Cara chose to join Team in Training (one of the first and best running charity groups, benefitting The Leukemia & Lymphoma Society). She says: "Looking back, it was one of my best moves. I looked forward to seeing everyone at workouts, and they motivated me to stick to the training."

But oops, poor Nadia: "I ran my first half without a plan. The most I had ever run before was 5 miles. I hurt for about a week and half after the race."

I'm not going to promise that you will cross the finish line feeling like you had a butterfly escort, but most runners—especially new runners—will feel better and achieve more if they plan properly. I realize I may be preaching to the choir on this. If you weren't seeking a plan for your half marathon, you would not be reading this book.

NOVICE TRAINING PROGRAMS

Novice 1 Program

Week	Mon	Tue	Wed	Thu	Fri	Sat	Sun
1	Rest	3-mile run	2-mile run or cross	3-mile run	Rest	30 min cross	4-mile run
2	Rest	3-mile run	2-mile run or cross	3-mile run	Rest	30 min cross	4-mile run
3	Rest	3.5-mile run	2-mile run or cross	3.5-mile run	Rest	40 min cross	5-mile run
4	Rest	3.5-mile run	2-mile run or cross	3.5-mile run	Rest	40 min cross	5-mile run
5	Rest	4-mile run	2-mile run or cross	4-mile run	Rest	40 min cross	6-mile run
6	Rest	4-mile run	2-mile run or cross	4-mile run	Rest or easy run	Rest	5K race
7	Rest	4.5-mile run	3-mile run or cross	4.5-mile run	Rest	50 min cross	7-mile run
8	Rest	4.5-mile run	3-mile run or cross	4.5-mile run	Rest	50 min cross	8-mile run
9	Rest	5-mile run	3-mile run or cross	5-mile run	Rest or easy run	Rest	10K race
10	Rest	5-mile run	3-mile run or cross	5-mile run	Rest	60 min cross	9-mile run
11	Rest	5-mile run	3-mile run or cross	5-mile run	Rest	60 min cross	10-mile run
12	Rest	4-mile run	3-mile run or cross	2-mile run	Rest	Rest	Half marathon

Novice 2 Program

Week	Mon	Tue	Wed	Thu	Fri	Sat	Sun
1	Rest	3-mile run	3-mile run	3-mile run	Rest	4-mile run	60 min cross
2	Rest	3-mile run	3-mile pace	3-mile run	Rest	5-mile run	60 min cross
3	Rest	3-mile run	4-mile run	3-mile run	Rest	6-mile run	60 min cross
4	Rest	3-mile run	4-mile pace	3-mile run	Rest	7-mile run	60 min cross
5	Rest	3-mile run	4-mile run	3-mile run	Rest	8-mile run	60 min cross
6	Rest	3-mile run	4-mile pace	3-mile run	Rest	5K race	60 min cross
7	Rest	3-mile run	5-mile run	3-mile run	Rest	9-mile run	60 min cross
8	Rest	3-mile run	5-mile pace	3-mile run	Rest	10-mile run	60 min cross
9	Rest	3-mile run	5-mile run	3-mile run	Rest	10K race	60 min cross
10	Rest	3-mile run	5-mile pace	3-mile run	Rest	11-mile run	60 min cross
11	Rest	3-mile run	5-mile run	3-mile run	Rest	12-mile run	60 min cross
12	Rest	3-mile run	2-mile pace	3-mile run	Rest	Rest	Half marathon

Note: To convert English distances to metric, use an online conversion website such as www.onlineconversion.com/length_common.

The differences between these two novice programs are subtle, but important. The weekly (thus total) mileage for novice 1 is slightly lower than for novice 2, but only slightly. Week 1 of novice 1 features 10 to 12 miles (16-19 km); week 1 of novice 2 features 13 miles (21 km). Week 11 (the peak week) of novice 1 features 20 to 23 miles (32-37 km). Week 11 of novice 2 features 23 miles (37 km). But if you only look at total miles, you are missing the point. The difference between the two novice programs comes from what you do with those miles. The second program contains more *quality* miles.

How Novice 1 Works

Let's begin by defining the workouts for novice 1.

Rest

When you begin novice 1, the first workout you encounter on Monday (and all Mondays) is rest. It may seem counterproductive to consider rest a workout, but rest is as important a part of your training as the running. You will be able to run the long runs on the weekend better—and limit your risk of injury—if you rest before them on Fridays and rest after them on Mondays. Rest thus brackets the cross-training and long runs on Saturdays and Sundays, when runners have more free time to devote to their training. Bracketed weekends is at the heart of all my training programs.

Run

When you see the word run in any of my programs, that means I want you to run at a conversational pace. I mentioned this in the chapter on base training, and I'll mention it again here because this is important: Don't worry about how fast you run your regular workouts. The numbers that various electronic devices spit at us during our workouts (and afterward) are fun, but don't become trapped by them. If you're training with a friend, the two of you should be able to hold a conversation without getting out of breath. If you can't do that, you're running too fast, perhaps trying to keep up with a faster runner who should be slowing down for you. Be aware also that your conversational pace might be different from one day to another, depending on what you did the day before. Tuesday's run might be easiest (and fastest) after a day of rest on Monday. Thursday's run might be hardest (and slowest) because it's your second or third day in a row of running. (For those wearing heart rate monitors, your target zone probably should be between 65 and 75 percent of your maximum pulse rate. One reason to wear a heart monitor is that it takes the decision making out of your hands when it comes to picking an easy pace.) One other consideration. Often you encounter a day—sun shining, cool rather than warm, beautiful scenery, wind at your back regardless of which direction you run—so perfect that there is no excuse to hold back. I will not be standing by the side of the road to trip you. Running should be fun. At the same time, a program is a program. Following it pretty close to "precisely" will help you achieve all your goals. Keep that in mind so you don't deviate from the program too frequently.

Distance

The novice 1 training schedule features workouts at distances from 2 to 10 miles (4.8-16 km). Don't worry about running precisely those distances, but you should come close. Pick a course through the neighborhood or in some scenic area where you think you might enjoy running. Then measure the course either by car or bicycle. In deciding where to train, talk to other runners. They probably can point you to accurately measured courses for your workouts. GPS watches seemingly make measuring courses easy, but trees and tall buildings can temporarily interfere with their accuracy. Also, don't be afraid to use educated guesses when it comes to determining how fast you just ran. If you normally run at a 10:00 pace (6:12/km), and you come in after running a half hour, you probably ran about 3 miles (4.8 km). *Probably* works for me; it should work for you.

Cross-Train

When you see *cross* on any of my schedules, it means cross-train. What form of cross-training works best? It could be swimming, cycling, walking, cross-country skiing, snowshoeing, in other words, exercises that are aerobic, meaning they stress your cardiovascular system. What cross-training you select depends on your personal preference. But don't make the mistake of cross-training too vigorously. Sports such as basketball or volleyball that involve sideways motions or sudden stops and starts do not, in my mind, qualify as cross-training. In fact, you may increase your risk of injury if you double up on these sports, particularly as the mileage builds. Novice 1 suggests that you cross-train on Saturday before your long run, but you could just as easily flip-flop days and run long on Saturdays. In week 1, cross-train for a half hour, gradually increasing to a full hour in weeks 10 and 11. On Wednesdays, you have the option of doing a short run or cross-training.

How long should each cross-training workout last? For the weekend cross-training workouts, I usually suggest the number of minutes. Please note use of the word "suggest." Don't get hung up on specific time limits. Exercises such as swimming, cycling, and walking are different enough from running, so it is difficult to compare one workout to another. If I prescribe 60 minutes, I mean "about an hour." On days when I offer you the option to

Swimming is a good form of cross-training because it is an aerobic exercise.

cross-train or run, determine how long it would take you to run the distance prescribed, then cross-train for about that same length of time. I'll continue to say more about cross-training in later chapters.

Long Runs

The most important workout of the week comes on Sundays in this program: the long run, progressively increasing in distance each weekend. Over a period of 12 weeks, your longest run will increase from 4 miles (6.4 km) in week 1 to 10 miles (16 km) in week 11. Don't worry about making the final jump from 10 miles in practice to 13.1 miles in the race. Inspiration will carry you to the finish line, plus the final week features a taper to ensure you are well rested going into the race. The schedule suggests doing your long runs on Sundays, but you can do them on Saturdays or any other convenient day, if necessary.

Walking

Walking is an excellent exercise that a lot of runners overlook in their training. I don't specify walking breaks, but feel free to walk during your running workouts any time you feel tired or need to shift gears. Let me offer a nod in the direction of fellow friend and guru, Jeff Galloway, who popularized the use of walking breaks both in workouts and in races. (Thank you, Jeff.) When you go to the starting line in your 12th week, nobody will care whether you run every step of the half marathon; they're more concerned that you finish! If this means walking every step in practice and in the race, do it! Be aware that I also offer a separate half marathon training program for those who plan to walk all the way (see chapter 13).

Races

In week 6 and again in week 9, I suggest that you consider entering a running race at a relatively short distance: a 5K or a 10K. If you never have experienced a running race before, the thought of running 13.1 miles in the company of 10,000 or more runners may seem intimidating. One way to dispel your nervousness is to dip your toes in the water without jumping in. Choose a local 5K, one without too many people or too high an entry fee. Wait a couple of weeks and test yourself in another race, maybe a 10K. Each race is different, and a lot of psychic energy is generated in the biggest ones, so you might as well get an idea of what to expect. If you can't find races at the prescribed distances on the day of the week suggested, or in the week suggested, feel free to modify the schedule. Notice that I prescribe one or two days of rest on Friday and Saturday before the Sunday races as well as a rest day on Monday for recovery afterward. For Saturday races, shift the rest days accordingly.

Juggling

Don't be afraid to juggle the workouts from day to day and week to week. If you have an important business meeting on Thursday, do that workout on Wednesday instead. If your family is going to be on vacation one week when · you will have more or less time to train, adjust the schedule accordingly. If your vacation includes hiking, skiing, biking, or some other fun activity, you have my permission to consider it cross-training. Be consistent with your training, and the overall details won't matter. Having said that, I know that many of my followers take great pride in following my programs *exactly* as written. And I can understand the confidence that this builds in them.

How Novice 2 Works

How does novice 2 differ from novice 1? Not much. As stated already, the mileage totals—both weekly and total—are almost the same, the differences from one day to the other being so trivial that it is almost not worth mentioning them. In week 1, for instance, you run 3 miles (4.8 km) instead of 2 miles (3.2 km) on Wednesday, and I fail to suggest a cross-training option on that day, although runners certainly are welcome to take one. But, hey, novice 1 runners actually run more miles on Tuesdays and Thursdays than do novice 2 runners: Aren't we moving backward?

Not really, because Wednesdays in novice 2 feature somewhat tougher workouts than the Wednesdays of novice 1. Some of the mileage lost from Tuesdays and Thursdays has been moved to Wednesday. There is also a tantalizing word not found in the novice 1 schedule. It is *pace*. Yikes! Every other Wednesday features a pace run rather than simply a run run, if you follow me. I told you earlier that when I say run, I mean for you to run at a conversational pace. At the risk of confusing you, when I now say pace, I mean for you to run at the pace you plan to run in your goal half marathon, thus half marathon pace.

Important reasoning stands behind this strategy. You want to teach your body to recognize race pace. If you plan to run the half marathon at 8:00 per mile (4:58/km), or 9:00 per mile (5:35/km), or 10:00 per mile (6:12/km) or any number of minutes and seconds per mile, you want to know what that pace feels like. *Exactly* what that pace feels like. The worst mistake any competitor can make in a road race is to run the first mile or two at a pace that is too fast, which usually results in a pace that is too slow in the last mile or two, often a disastrously slow, struggle-home pace and a disappointing final time. Experienced runners know this and benefit from practicing their pace.

Might not first-time half-marathoners (those who chose novice 1) benefit from practicing race pace? Yes, but they do not know what that pace might be because they have not run and finished their first half marathon. Doing so not only allows them the right to paste a 13.1 sticker on their back bumper, but they also acquire the knowledge to train with a higher degree of sophistication for future races. This is a rite of passage that all novice runners eventually earn, allowing them to move from novice 1 to novice 2.

A couple of other small differences are that novice 2 runners cross-train on Sundays rather than Saturdays. Long runs shift to Saturdays, for no particular reason other than it feels right for me, the coach. (Don't argue with the coach.) I leave the type of aerobic activity undefined, but continue to favor swimming, cycling, and walking. The cross-training time prescription (60 minutes) remains the same for Sundays during the full length of the program. As for mileage, the difference between the long runs for novice 1 or novice 2 on the weekends is so slight as to almost be unnoticeable, but novice 2 runners begin at the same level (4 miles [6.4 km]) in week 1, but reach a higher level (12 miles [19 km]) in the penultimate week 11.

How fast can you run using one of my half marathon programs? That is a question impossible to answer, because it depends entirely on ability. Just as some athletes are better basketball players because they are tall, or are better football players because they are large, or are better baseball players because of good eye–hand coordination, some runners are better at our sport because they are light on their feet. Much of our success is genetic, although it helps to have a good training program and a willingness to follow it with dedication.

"Regardless of genetics," writes Luke Humphrey in *Hansons Half Marathon Method,* "training remains a vital predictor of running performance. Although genetics dictate what kind of work you may be innately suited for, the right training helps you maximize your individual potential" (Humphrey et al. 1991, p. 26). Either of my novice programs will get you to the finish line, and get you to that line more comfortably than if you did not have a plan.

11 | Moving Upward

From a runner's standpoint," claims Jack Daniels, PhD, in *Daniels' Running Formula*, "consistency in training is the single most important thing that leads to success. That consistency comes from concentrating on the task at hand—neither dwelling on the past nor looking too far forward. The only thing you can control is the present, and when you focus on that and remain consistent in your training, you'll find your greatest success" (Daniels 2014, p. 11).

Good point, Jack, and I couldn't agree more. Interacting with runners on the Internet, I frequently preach the benefits of consistency, almost to the point that I could use an extra key on my computer keyboard: One click and the word *consistency* would pop into my responses to training questions.

This became apparent when recently I asked my friends on Facebook to list their secrets of success. The word *consistency* bounced right back at me. Among those who used the word was Ellen Boettrich of Rochester, New York. Ellen's secrets were "Consistency. Patience. Cross-training. Rest days. Massage. Foam rolling. Intervals. Tempo runs. Strength training. Yoga. Running easy for most weekly mileage. Allowing for recovery regularly." That's practically a table of contents for this book. Almost as an afterthought Ellen added "Oh, and keeping training age appropriate. I'm 65."

Lionel Burnett, 54, a technology manager from Fort Smith, Arkansas, also underlined the importance of consistency before going on to say "Run very hard on hard days. Run very easy on easy days. Never skip the long run. Run five days a week and cross-train as well."

Hmmmm. That sounds suspiciously close to the new training program I am about to unveil for those who successfully finished a half marathon or two or three using one of the novice programs outlined in the previous chapter. In this chapter, I plan to show you how to move up to an intermediate program.

We are now going to take a half step upward. But only a half step. Richard Ansara, 42, a software engineer from Cincinnati, provides all the reason I need: "It was your intermediate half marathon plan that elevated my game. It shaved 16 minutes off of my time, allowing me to break two hours."

Time out. Pause. Wait a minute. I just got through endorsing consistency as the secret to success. That being the case, shouldn't runners simply select a program, whether novice, intermediate, or advanced, and stay there for the rest of their running lives? No, because unless you are an exceptional athlete and have a background of high school competition in track or cross country or both, my advanced programs will break you, and so may the intermediate ones. You don't achieve peak performance after only 12 weeks following a Hal Higdon program, or the program of any coach. The wisest of wise runners first choose an easy level—say novice 1 or novice 2—train consistently, then, and only then, are they ready to start moving upward.

Ginger Herring was among the wise ones. But also credit her coach. "I had a good coach (Joe Burgasser) who increased my mileage very slowly," says Herring, 72, from St. Petersburg, Florida. "He introduced some 5K races when he thought I was ready. Once I became used to one level, we would bump it up to the next. Learning the difference from not being able to run a session to not wanting to run a session is also a good tip." Herring was among those who identified consistency as definitely a key to her performance improvements.

Still, if you truly are interested in improvement—knocking a few minutes off your PR or simply learning how to train more comfortably—you sometimes need to move up. Thus, welcome to intermediate 1—and also intermediate 2.

My training programs for runners at various levels and for various race distances have been available free on the Internet for several decades. When writing a new book such as this one, the temptation is to rewrite, to invent, to innovate, to offer new ideas. Nevertheless, sometimes the old ideas are best. Let me quote my introduction to intermediate half, available for years on my website, halhigdon.com:

> "The Intermediate Half Marathon Training Program is for experienced runners: individuals who have left their novice roots behind and who want to improve their performances. You should be capable of running 30 to 60 minutes a day, five to seven days a week, have competed in at least a few 5K and 10K races, if not a marathon, and at least be willing to consider the possibility that some speed work might help you improve."

Benefits of Moving Up

Is moving upward (the title of this chapter) necessary? Does a compulsion cause runners to want to do a little bit more, to train just a tad harder as they go from half marathon number 1 to half marathon number 2 to 3 and beyond? The benefits of moving up are faster times and presumably more enjoyment, the thrill that comes with self-improvement. These runners found that to be true.

Barbara Farr claims to only have been running less than two years: "I participated in a training program through a running store over the summer for a first half marathon in the fall. I started with the beginner training. I am now at the end of a second program through the same place, but stepped it up to intermediate, aimed at a spring half. More miles weekly and longer runs on Saturday so far have improved my pace and performance. Speed work this time around and having more knowledge as well when it comes to fueling also have helped. I hope to PR at my second half marathon in May."

Pete DiAngelis, Jr., favored speed over endurance when he trained for his most recent half marathon. He now says "The added speed work associated with intermediate 2 will make you faster than the long runs alone. I'm finally getting a grasp on the importance of knowing when to run fast and knowing when to not run fast."

Here's that word consistency again, as applied by Daniel Kiewel: "I think the biggest things for me have been consistency, increasing mileage slightly without overtraining, and most importantly the incorporation of strength training into my workouts!"

But Stuart Perkins offers another approach that other endurance athletes might consider. Stuart says he never actually trains for half marathons: "I run them as part of my marathon training." (Given that all my 18-week full marathon training programs suggest a half in week 8 or week 9, this is easy for many to do.) Stuart says "I find that the longer, slow runs required in the marathon training prepare me well for the half distance."

That's the old, but let me introduce you to the new: the rollout of a new training program for runners at the intermediate level. (Drum roll, maestro.) I have labels for these two programs: intermediate 1 and intermediate 2. Intermediate 1 is the new program, while the previous intermediate has been renamed intermediate 2.

The Ramp

For those who begin at the beginning, a definite ramp leads upward in all my programs. In seeking improvements, I never ask runners to make sudden jumps. That is the road to perdition, not to mention injury and overtraining. In my half marathon programs, starting from when I first made them available online, the ramp leading up from novice to intermediate to advanced was steady and logical. Up. Up. Up. But now I have added a fork in the road. You need to make a choice. There are now two intermediates. One places the emphasis on endurance. The other focuses more on speed. Intermediate 1 and intermediate 2 sit side by side on a plateau. The two programs are equal. One is not more difficult than the other. They exist at the same level in separate universes. Just like Earth 1 and Earth 2 in a superhero comic book. Superman and Batman exist in both mythical worlds, but they are (slightly) different Supermans and Batmans.

Keep this in mind when you consider which program to choose as you move upward. Here's the difference, and it should be easy to understand as we compare the two programs: intermediate 1 and intermediate 2. Intermediate 1 is an endurance-based program; intermediate 2 is a speed-based program. Intermediate 1 adds more miles; intermediate 2 adds a day of speed work. One does not necessarily offer a greater challenge than another. You might select intermediate 1 because you have no interest in doing (and may even fear) speed work. You might select intermediate 2 because you think speed work might be fun, plus several respected coaches (Jack Daniels being one of them) suggest that speed work can help you improve your half marathon time. Or you might select intermediate 1 one time and intermediate 2 another without any desire to move beyond that level in my menu of programs before making the final leap to advanced.

Let's begin with intermediate 1 and describe how it differs from the novice programs presented in the previous chapter.

Hill training is an effective form of speedwork.

Control and Endurance

"Pilates, like running, is a way of life for me," says Christa Rogers, 52, a part-time nurse from Ocean Shores, Washington. As part of her job, Rogers teaches Pilates. The exercise regimen gets its name from Joseph Pilates, a German-born physical fitness devotee, who a century ago after studying yoga, invented a system of exercises, some of them using equipment, some of them using movement on mats. Pilates, which is practiced around the world, improves flexibility, builds strength, and develops control and endurance in the entire body.

Rogers offers her endorsement: "Developing core strength with Pilates has been a lifesaver, keeping me injury-free as I run." She suggests that Pilates offers benefits at all levels. A beginner can work out next to someone who has been practicing Pilates for years.

Living in a rural area, Rogers does not have access to a gym, so she works out using mats: "I only became an instructor because there were no classes available for me. I find Pilates the perfect complement to running, since it loosens those darn tight hamstrings. It stretches and strengthens muscles and also improves posture. The principles of Pilates are centering, concentration, control, fluidity, precision, and breathing. It differs from yoga in that poses are not held for any length of time."

Given my strict definition of cross-training as a workout that is aerobic, does Pilates qualify? Based on Rogers' description, it sounds like such a workout lasting a half hour or more in a gym would offer enough of an aerobic buzz to satisfy me. But does it matter what labels I put on an exercise? Go ahead and do it!

INTERMEDIATE TRAINING PROGRAMS

Intermediate 1 Program

Week	Mon	Tue	Wed	Thu	Fri	Sat	Sun
1	30 min cross	3-mile run	4-mile run	3-mile run	Rest	3-mile run	4-mile run
2	30 min cross	3-mile run	4-mile run	3-mile run	Rest	3-mile pace	5-mile run
3	40 min cross	3.5-mile run	5-mile run	3.5-mile run	Rest	Rest	6-mile run
4	40 min cross	3.5-mile run	5-mile run	3.5-mile run	Rest	3-mile run	7-mile run
5	40 min cross	4-mile run	6-mile run	4-mile run	Rest	3-mile pace	8-mile run
6	50 min cross	4-mile run	6-mile run	4-mile run	Rest or easy run	Rest	5K race
7	Rest	4.5-mile run	7-mile run	4.5-mile run	Rest	4-mile pace	9-mile run
8	50 min cross	4.5-mile run	7-mile run	4.5-mile run	Rest	5-mile pace	10-mile run
9	60 min cross	5-mile run	8-mile run	5-mile run	Rest or easy run	Rest	10K race
10	Rest	5-mile run	8-mile run	5-mile run	Rest	5-mile pace	11-mile run
11	60 min cross	5-mile run	6-mile run	4-mile run	Rest	3-mile pace	12-mile run
12	Rest	4-mile run	4-mile run	2-mile run	Rest	Rest	Half marathon

Intermediate 2 Program

Week	Mon	Tue	Wed	Thu	Fri	Sat	Sun
1	30 min cross	3-mile run	5 × 400 m at 5K pace	3-mile run	Rest	3-mile run	5-mile run
2	30 min cross	3-mile run	30 min tempo	3-mile run	Rest	3-mile pace	6-mile run
3	40 min cross	3.5-mile run	6 × 400 m at 5K pace	3-mile run	Rest	Rest	5K race
4	40 min cross	3.5-mile run	35 min tempo	3-mile run	Rest	3-mile run	7-mile run
5	40 min cross	4-mile run	7 × 400 m at 5K pace	3-mile run	Rest	3-mile pace	8-mile run
6	50 min cross	4-mile run	40 min tempo	3-mile run	Rest or easy run	Rest	10K race
7	Rest	4.5-mile run	8 × 400 m at 5K pace	3-mile run	Rest	4-mile pace	9-mile run
8	50 min cross	4.5-mile run	40 min tempo	3-mile run	Rest	5-mile pace	10-mile run
9	60 min cross	5-mile run	9 × 400 m at 5K pace	3-mile run	Rest or easy run	Rest	15K race
10	Rest	5-mile run	45 min tempo	3-mile run	Rest	5-mile pace	11-mile run
11	60 min cross	5-mile run	10 × 400 m at 5K pace	3-mile run	Rest	3-mile pace	12-mile run
12	Rest	4-mile run	30 min tempo	2-mile run	Rest	Rest	Half marathon

Note: To convert English distances to metric, use an online conversion website such as www.onlineconversion.com/length_common.

How Intermediate 1 Works

Cross-Training

In the novice programs, I prescribe cross-training, listed as cross, for Saturdays or Sundays. Intermediate runners cross-train on Mondays, gradually increasing the time given that activity from 30 minutes in week 1 to 60 minutes in week 11, the penultimate week before the half marathon. What sports are best for cross-training? Aerobic sports such as swimming, cycling, walking, and cross-country skiing top my list. Turn back to page 107 to read what I previously said about cross-training for the novice programs. Then flip forward to chapter 14 for more on the subject.

Run

The runs on Tuesdays and Thursdays and sometimes Saturdays are listed as run, and they are designed to be done at a comfortable pace: an easy pace, an I'm-not-yet-out-of-breath pace. If you're wearing a heart rate monitor, you should stay in the 65 to 75 percent zone, but you really don't need an electronic device to tell you when you're running easy. Run means you just run at whatever pace allows you to enjoy the scenery. If you're feeling good, can you pick up the pace toward the end? Yes, but don't get overconfident. The reason I want you to run easy on Tuesdays is because I'm going to ask you to run harder on Wednesdays, and by Thursday's workouts you may be tired enough that you will be happy to obey what I say and stay at what might be described as midweek easy.

Midweek

Wednesday is a hard day in my intermediate programs. Not *the* hard day, because that comes on the weekends, but somewhat harder than the two days on each side. If you are familiar with my marathon training programs, this is the day on which I ask runners training to race 26.2 to do a *sorta-long* run. Not as long as the long runs, but definitely longer than the short runs. Intermediate 1 runners embrace these sorta-long runs midweek, beginning with 4 miles (6.4 km) in week 1 and peaking with 8 miles (13 km) in weeks 9 and 10. (The sorta-long run in week 11 drops back to 6 miles [9.6 km], because the taper leading up to the half marathon in week 12 has begun.) Wednesday on each of my intermediate programs provides one of the differences between the two intermediate programs. Intermediate 2 features speed work. More on that follows.

Rest

Friday on almost all of my programs is a day of rest. The reason for this should be obvious. You will be able to train more effectively on the weekends if you are well rested. This allows you to get a good night's sleep, so that you are well rested when you roll out of bed early Saturday and Sunday mornings. I suspect some of the advanced runners are going to grumble and moan when I tell them to take a day off on Friday, but, being an intermediate runner, you are more mellow when it comes to following my advice.

Pace

That term used in any of my programs relates to the pace you plan to run in your goal race, in this case half marathon pace. If you plan to run 10:00 (6:12/km) pace in your half en route to a finish around 2:10 or 2:15, this is how fast you run in workouts described as pace. The purpose is to familiarize yourself with that pace so that you don't make a mistake by going out too fast or too slow in the first 2 miles (3.2 km) of your race. Going out too fast, by the way, is a much worse error than going out too slow. If you go out too slow in the first few miles, you probably can make up time lost in the next few miles. Go out too fast, and you may be reduced to walking toward the end. To prevent that, we practice pace. This may require training over a course with mile markers or trusting the GPS watch that you bought for more than you can afford in the running specialty store. GPS watches provide good data, but not necessarily perfect data. You have 12 weeks to teach your body how to pace yourself correctly in your goal half marathon. That's not always easy, but you identified yourself as an already experienced runner by deciding to follow this program. I trust you to succeed. If you never have run a half marathon before, or have not run one recently, you may not know what to expect in your race. There are numerous prediction programs available online that allow you to insert past race times at various distances from 5K to the marathon and obtain a good estimate of what goal time (and pace) to choose. *Runner's World* offers such a prediction program on its website, RunnersWorld.com; I often send runners to the programs offered by coach, Greg McMillan, at McMillanRunning.com.

Long Runs

The most important workout in any endurance-based program is the long run, done on Sundays for intermediate 1 and 2 runners. The former begin at 4 miles (6.4 km) in week 1 and peak at 12 miles (19 km) (1.1 miles short of half marathon distance) in week 11. The latter start slightly longer at 5 miles (8 km), but also peak at 12 miles (19 km). I tell those following my full marathon schedules to do their long runs 30 to 90 seconds or more slower than race pace, and that advice works well for you, too. Your pace should be conversational, similar to the easy runs midweek. Don't be heroic. Don't turn your long runs into races with those around you or against your watch. (The watch always wins.) If you run too hard on the weekend, you won't have enough energy to handle workouts in the middle of the week. The schedule outlined earlier suggests doing your long runs on Sundays. You can do them Saturdays if that day seems more convenient, but it is easier to do a long run the day after a pace run than vice versa. Incidentally, use your long runs to practice nutrition: both the food and fluids you imbibe during the run and before. Don't cruise through mile 2 in the half marathon and suddenly realize you can't tolerate the sport drink offered. Usually you can find out which sports drink a specific race will offer you on the course by going to the race's website.

Walking

Walking is an excellent exercise that a lot of runners overlook in their training. I don't specify walking breaks, but feel free to walk during your running workouts any time you feel tired or need to shift gears. And if you come to a red traffic light, for Pete's sake, don't jog in place. You may feel you need to keep jogging to keep your heart rate up, but that is not really necessary. You can rest without guilt. Use the time spent waiting for the light to change to do some easy stretching. Since most runners probably fail to do enough stretching because it takes time, taking a stoplight break or two probably is a good idea. Regardless, stop. Wait. Look both ways after the light turns green. In coaching marathon runners, I usually recommend that they walk through the aid stations to allow them to drink more. If you want to walk at prescribed time intervals—say five minutes running and one minute walking—that is fine, too. Also, don't overlook walking as a cross-training exercise. And it could be something as simple as a stroll in the park with your spouse, or pushing a stroller rather than power walking.

Racing

Most experienced runners enjoy racing, so I've included two races during the training period for intermediate 1 runners and three races for intermediate 2 runners. I chose a logical progression from 5K to 10K to 15K, but there is nothing magic about those particular distances. Plug in whatever races look interesting in your local area wherever they fit in your schedule. As suggested a few pages ago, you can use races to test your fitness and, using an online prediction chart, to predict your finishing time in the half marathon and thus a prediction of the pace you have some chance running in your goal race. Speaking of pace, any time you run a specific pace in a race at any distance, you refine your skills at pacing yourself in half marathons, too.

How Intermediate 2 Works

Speed Work: Interval Training

Here is where intermediate 2 differs greatly from intermediate 1. As I wrote earlier, intermediate 1 is an endurance-based training program; intermediate 2 is speed based. If you are comfortable doing interval workouts on the track and tempo runs in the woods (and not all runners are), you can significantly improve your speed, which will translate into faster race times. An interval workout usually consists of fast repeats separated by walking or jogging breaks. Intermediate 2 begins with 5 × 400 meters in week 1 and adds one more 400 every other week to reach 10 × 400 meters in week 11. Walk or jog between each repeat. The best place to run 400-meter repeats is on a track, although you can also use an accurately measured road course or even use a time-based approach on the roads or on a treadmill: two minutes fast, then two minutes slow, for instance. Run the 400s at about your pace for 5K or 10K.

Speed Work: Tempo Runs

A tempo run is a continuous run with a buildup in the middle to near 10K race pace. A tempo run of 30 to 45 minutes would begin with 10 to 15 minutes of easy running, building to 15 to 20 minutes of fast running near the middle, then 5 to 10 minutes easy toward the end. The pace buildup should be gradual, not sudden, with peak speed coming about two-thirds into the workout. You do not need to run the increments at a specific speed or over a specific distance. I prefer doing tempo runs in the woods, my favorite course being trails in Indiana Dunes State Park, near the town of Chesterton. Tempo runs are my favorite workouts. I hope they become yours, too.

Who can best benefit from either of these training programs? Again it comes down to the words from Jack Daniels that I used to open this chapter: "Consistency in training is the single most important thing that leads to success." Consistency is an approach that also works well for those moving further up to the advanced program.

12 | The Pinnacle

Whitney Zeka-McFadden, 42, a pharmaceutical representative from Edmond, Oklahoma, could not understand the reasons for her improvement as a runner. She admitted to being perplexed: "After years of long runs, multiple half marathons and several full marathons, my job situation put me in a spot where I had to reduce the time I devoted to long runs, particularly those time-draining workouts on weekends. So I cut back on my miles, running 4-milers (6.4 km) every day that I could, and as fast as I could, for about six months. Keeping it short, I still managed five workouts a week. Then, things got back to normal, and I increased one of my runs, adding 2 miles (3.2 km) to it for four weeks, which put me at 12 miles (19 km) just before I ran a half marathon. *Boom!* Broke two hours, and a year later, I'm still faster. Not only that, I shaved a minute off my full marathon pace! Riddle me that."

Easy riddle to solve, Whitney. First, you changed your training pattern. You did something entirely different, which is always a good idea when caught in a training rut. You cut miles. Shorter runs resulted in faster runs, a form of speed work, although nothing like the traditional interval training on the track or hill repeats on the road. And while long runs and high weekly mileage remain an important part of any training program, running long and slow all the time can deaden the legs and rob runners of the ability to run fast—or at least prevent them from running faster.

Thus the answer to Whitney's riddle: If you want to achieve success, you need to master the arts of speed and endurance and blend them into a single training program. That's how to reach the pinnacle.

Running More Aggressively

How do you improve as a runner? How do you shatter personal records? How do you feel comfortable both in the race and during those weekend long runs we love? After reviewing his training notes before a recent half marathon, Brian Galhouse, 43, a project manager from Fairfax, Virginia, offers his take on the subject:

1. The long runs leading up to the half were 16 (25.7 km) and 17 miles (27.3 km), so I was positive I could attack the distance with confidence. Knowing that a failure to finish was largely a nonissue allowed me to focus on running a bit more aggressively than in the past.

2. The speed work really clicked for me. I had done some speed work while training for previous races, but the tempo runs on Thursdays peaking at 60 minutes gave me the courage to break away from the pace group, knowing I would not die after a short midrace sprint. It also allowed me to relax while waiting in the crowded starting corral.

3. Trusting my body signals also set me up for success. I resisted the temptation to look at my watch. I paid close attention to my body and ran as hard as it would let me. Checking my splits later, I found that I had run within 1 or 2 percent of perfect pace without obsessing over my watch. This helped me greatly in a later full marathon.

Reaching the pinnacle is not easy, but it is also not difficult if you understand the principles of training—what works and what does not work. "All it really takes to perform up to our full potential," instructs Roy Benson, author of *Coach Benson's "Secret" Workouts: Coachly Wisdom for Runners About Effort-Based Training*, "is following a training program that offers frequent workouts at a moderately hard effort on a consistent basis" (Benson 2003, p.73).

Frequent workouts. Moderately hard. Pay attention everybody. This is an *aha* moment. The five runs a week that Whitney Zeka-McFadden did regularly certainly qualified as frequent workouts. Four miles at a somewhat faster pace than Whitney had run before also meets Coach Benson's definition of moderately hard.

Other runners, perhaps without realizing it, have followed in the footsteps of Zeka-McFadden, mixing speed with distance, or at least they trotted along on parallel paths. Kathy Gollenbusch Walker, 47, an accountant from Five Oak, California, improved by adding interval training and hill repeats to her workout mix, but adds "More important for me was a sudden mindset that I wanted more speed and distance. A friend said casually to me one day, 'You gotta want it.' I chewed on her remark for a day or two and decided, yeah, I really did want it. After that, I never looked back."

Stephanie Gledhill, 36, a local government manager from Leeds, England, claims to have gotten faster after joining a running club. "Running with faster people makes you faster yourself," says Gledhill. "You have to believe you can run faster and learn to run in pain: not injured pain, just-out-of-your-comfort-zone pain. It's amazing how much faster you can be when you believe and keep up the pace." Gledhill ran her first half in just over two hours and has now cut her time by 15 minutes, admitting it took five years to achieve that level of improvement.

But wait a minute. Is there not something lurking in the woodpile, a form of training that scares both new runners and veteran runners, too, training that hurts, training that injures, training described in the classic motto on the T-shirts of high school cross country runners: *No pain, no gain.* Interesting motto, but I don't recall ever having seen a T-shirt that announced, "No moderately hard effort, no gain." Shudder!

Pain? Does hard training need to be painful, in which case many runners may (wisely) say, "I don't think I will apply." I am haunted by comments made by Timothy Noakes, MD, at the beginning of his landmark book, *Lore of Running.* Noakes writes about participating in crew (rowing) while at university and learning to embrace pain and discomfort. Racing flat out in an eight-person shell over a 2,000-meter course indeed can be painful. Crew is almost the ultimate anaerobic activity, like running 400 meters in a track meet. Noakes later would compare his experiences as a rower to his experiences as a runner, having switched to the latter sport after earning his medical degree: "Rowing first introduced me to my need for self-inflicted pain—the special nauseating deep-seated pain that accompanies repetitive interval training and racing" (Noakes 2001, p. ix).

Okay, very poetic, Timmy, but does training at the top level, at the pinnacle, guarantee runners a life of pain? I might argue that it does not, particularly if you train intelligently—which means you do not overtrain. I feel reasonably sure that Timothy Noakes, MD, despite his quote just offered, would agree with me. As we shift from the two intermediate programs outlined in the previous chapter to the single advanced program that forms the core of this one, I am going to suggest that just because you train at the pinnacle, it does not mean you leave the comfort of novice and intermediate behind for the pain of advanced.

ADVANCED TRAINING PROGRAM

Week	Mon	Tue	Wed	Thu	Fri	Sat	Sun
1	3-mile run	6 × hill	3-mile run	40 min tempo	Rest	3-mile run	1:30 run (3/1)
2	3-mile run	7 × 400 m at 5K pace	3-mile run	45 min tempo	Rest	3-mile pace	1:30 run
3	3-mile run	7 × hill	3-mile run	30 min tempo	Rest or easy run	Rest	5K race
4	3-mile run	8 × 400 m at 5K pace	3-mile run	40 min tempo	Rest	3-mile run	1:30 run (3/1)
5	3-mile run	8 × hill	3-mile run	45 min tempo	Rest	3-mile pace	1:30 min run
6	3-mile run	8 × 400 m at 5K pace	3-mile run	30 min tempo	Rest or easy run	Rest	10K race
7	3-mile run	4 × 800 m at 10K pace	3-mile run	45 min tempo	Rest	4-mile pace	1:45 run (3/1)
8	3-mile run	3 × 1,600 m at race pace	3-mile run	50 min tempo	Rest	5-mile pace	1:45 run
9	3-mile run	5 × 800 m at 10K pace	3-mile run	30 min tempo	Rest or easy run	Rest	15K race
10	3-mile run	4 × 1,600 m at race pace	3-mile run	55 min tempo	Rest	5-mile pace	2:00 run (3/1)
11	3-mile run	6 × 800 m at 10K pace	3-mile run	60 min tempo	Rest	3-mile pace	2:00 run
12	3-mile run	6 × 400 m at 5K pace	3-mile run	30 min tempo	Rest	Rest	Half marathon

Note: To convert English distances to metric, use an online conversion website such as www.onlineconversion.com/length_common.

It is time to analyze the advanced training program day by day. Unlike my full marathon programs, I do not have an advanced 1 and advanced 2 half marathon program. Just one program at the half level. This is it: the pinnacle.

How the Advanced Program Works

Mondays

No more cross-training. I know advanced runners well enough to know that they want to focus their energy entirely on running. As an advanced runner, you don't want to waste your time riding a bike or swimming in a pool. You want to run! And, scientists tell us, because training at its top level is sport specific, running is what you need to do, not merely to improve, but to stay at your high level. If you get injured, I concede, you may be *forced* to cross-train, but other than that, you advanced runners, Run! Run! Run! *Cross* is a word that normally does not exist in the advanced runner's vocabulary.

Sure, this is advanced, the pinnacle, but you know I don't believe in overtraining. I continue to steal from the Bill Bowerman songbook of hard/easy. Ergo, the runs on Mondays, Wednesdays, and sometimes Fridays or Saturdays are intended to be done at a comfortable pace. Don't worry about how fast you run these workouts. *Run easy!* If you're training with a friend, the two of you should be able to hold a conversation. If you can't do that, you're running too fast. (For those wearing heart rate monitors, your target zone should be 65 to 75 percent of your maximum pulse rate.) If you slide above that on one of my prescribed easy runs, I will disown you.

In *Faster Road Racing*, coauthors Pete Pfitzinger and Philip Latter offer the scientific reason why rest often is best: "Recovery training improves blood flow to and from the muscles, speeding recovery and leaving you better prepared for your next hard workout. The increased blood flow brings in nutrients, helps remove waste products, and improves muscle repair. Short, easy recovery runs also provide an opportunity to rebuild your glycogen stores and contribute to your overall training volume and aerobic development" (Pfitzinger and Latter 2015, p. 37).

Thank you, Pete and Philip. When it comes to science, I bow to the scientists. When I say "run easy," I parrot what I learn from them. But a lot of my knowledge comes from the laboratory of the outdoors, every footstep that I have taken during a long running career.

What about activities other than running? Feel you need to do some strength training? I work out regularly in a gym and recommend pumping iron. You could strength train on almost any day of the week, but my recommendation would be to head to the gym on Mondays and Wednesdays. The distance doesn't change on these two days: 3 miles (4.8 km) on Mondays, 3 miles

Determining Maximum Heart Rate

Various formulas exist that allow runners to predict their maximum heart rates based on age. You can even find target heart rate calculators on the Internet. One formula is 220 minus your age, thus a 30-year-old should have an MHR of 190. But were that 30-year-old already a runner possessing a high level of fitness, a formula of 200 minus half the age might be accurate, thus 200 minus 15 equals an MHR of 185. There are various other formulas you can find on the Internet if you want to do a search for "maximum heart rate formula." But I can tell you that when I was that age and at the peak of my competitive ability, my MHR was 160, not calculated by some formula, but measured with precise accuracy during a treadmill run with exercise scientists peering over my shoulder. When you reach your max, the numbers which have been ascending all through your treadmill run suddenly plateau. The heart can't beat any faster or pump any more blood through your cardiovascular system to the muscles. At max, you might be able to run another minute or more at which point you either stop or get flipped off the end of the treadmill (and I saw this happen once during the test of a Norwegian runner in Oslo).

The formulas may be useful for most individuals, but not everyone. Sometimes I would get questions posted to me on the Internet from runners who tried to base their training on a target heart zone only to find that they couldn't push into that zone without getting hopelessly out of breath. Expecting to be at 65 to 75 percent of max, they might be at 85 to 95 percent of max. Not their fault; the formulas didn't work for them.

Unfortunately, not all physicians or scientists who offer treadmill tests want to push novice runners to their maximum for fear they might kill them. They stop short of max at the point where they have determined the individual is not going to trigger a heart attack by running. Can't say I blame them, but the test is not useful if your purpose was to determine MHR so you can base your training on it. That being the case, ask the individual supervising your test to allow you to reach your actual max, the point when your heartbeat numbers plateau. Another way to determine MHR is to run a 5K or 10K race and finish with a flat-out sprint. If the numbers shown on your GPS watch indicate a plateau in the last 10 to 15 seconds, then that is your max. Not all runners, however, have the ability to sprint at the end of a race. Their legs, rather than their hearts, may be the limiting factor. In that case, hope that the formulas work for you.

on Wednesdays. Use a 3-miler as a warm-up before your weight work. Is strength training going to make you a faster runner? If you could see me now, you would see me shrugging my shoulders, because I honestly do not know. I strength train because I believe it contributes to my longevity and ability to move at a somewhat faster pace than my age peers. Does that make me a faster runner? Yeah, I guess it does.

Tuesdays

This is one of the days when you do speed work, and here is where I explain 6 × hill and 7 × 400 m at 5K pace. Shortcut terms like that sometimes freak out people who come to our sport without having participated on a track or cross country team in high school or college. Hill training will help strengthen your quads and build speed. The workout on Tuesday in week 1 is 6 × hill.

That means you do a half dozen sprints up a hill. Look for a hill between 200 and 400 meters long. Jog or walk an equal distance between each repeat, usually going back down to the level on which you started your hill repeat. How steep should the hill be? It both does and does not matter. Pick your workout hill for convenience, not for the degree of its rise. If the hill is very steep, shorten the length of your sprint up it, perhaps only 200 meters or less. If the hill is gentle, you may want to lengthen your sprint. How fast? Think effort rather than seconds on a stopwatch. Let Coach Benson be your guide and run moderately hard.

The same might be said for interval training. By 7 × 400 m at 5K pace, I mean for you to run seven 400-meter repeats, each one a single lap on an outdoor track. Run these repetitions, or reps, at about the pace you would run in a 5K race. For the interval between the fast repeats, jog or walk a lap. During weeks 1 through 6, the distance for the fast repeats is 400 meters. Alternate every other week with the hill workouts. During weeks 7 through 12, the repeat

If you live in a flat state, use stadium steps for your hill training.

distances are 800 meters (two laps) and 1,600 meters (four laps), but use the same rest interval featured in the first half dozen weeks. You should be able to recover (i.e., lower your pulse rate from 85 to 95 percent down to 65 to 75 percent) during a single lap around the track. Too much rest during the interval between defeats the purpose of the training, which is to run faster than a normal pace run. Run the 800s at your 10K pace; run the 1,600s at your race pace for the half marathon. Yes, this all sounds complicated, but runners quickly adjust to interval training on a track. If not, consider employing the services of a coach to guide you into the interval training wilderness without bumping into too many trees.

Could you do this workout on the roads? Yes, you could. Run for the same length of time on the road that it would take you to run 400, 800, or 1,600 meters on the track. Rest accordingly. Could you do this workout on a treadmill? Yes, you could. Again use time to dictate your workout.

I prescribed only three hill sessions, all in the first half of the program, but if you want to do more hill training, be my guest. You can substitute hill repeats for any of the interval workouts, or even in place of a tempo run or two if you want. Olympic marathon champion Frank Shorter says that hill training is the equivalent of interval training, and I agree with Frank.

One other important point: Warm up before doing any speed training. Your first step on the track should not be a fast repeat. A good way to get injured is to stress muscles before they are warm. Jog a mile or two (1.6-2 km). Stretch. Visit the bathroom or grab a drink of water. Stretch. Do a handful of sprints the length of the football field in the middle of the track. Stretch. After the speed workout, cool down with additional easy running. This is the way that experienced track athletes do interval training, and we can learn from them. If you belong to a club that includes among its membership fast runners who use interval training, ask them about the warm-up and cool-down. Their 5- or 10-minute response may leave your eyeballs spinning, but if you pay close attention and are not afraid to ask them to repeat what they just said, you will benefit from this type of training.

Wednesdays

On the chart, the prescription is the same for the 12 Mondays and for the 12 Wednesdays, but let me offer you a chance to take a few steps away from your coach. Some runners compare the mileage between my novice, intermediate, and advanced programs and discover that some of the so-called easier programs (novice, intermediate) have more miles or nearly as many miles than the so-called more difficult programs (advanced). I don't know. I don't count miles. And those counting miles need to count the warm-up and cool-down miles mentioned earlier. It gets complicated. Yes, during the semi-elite phase of my running life, I kept careful track of how many miles I ran each day and each week. This was partly for motivational reasons. If I ran 100 miles (161 km) in a week, it helped build my confidence a nudge more than if I had only run 99 (159 km). Sometimes this focus on mileage, mileage, mileage got me into trouble. I feel that I am smarter now because of training errors suffered in the past. You get the benefit of this wisdom.

Quantity is not a panacea; quality must fit into the training picture, too. My advanced programs earn the advanced label because they feature quality more than quantity. The best programs, of course, balance quantity and quality.

Thus, if you want to combine quantity and quality, run a few miles more. An easy run of 3 miles (4.8 km) between the two speed workout days allows you to maintain the quality of those two sessions. Or you can add miles to the prescribed distance. Wednesday would be a good day to do so. Back up to the intermediate 1 schedule in chapter 11. The sorta-long run on Wednesdays starts at 4 miles (6.4 km) in week 1 and peaks at 8 miles (13 km) in week 10 before the taper begins. You could insert the Wednesday column from half intermediate 1 into half advanced, plugging a few miles into the program, but I'll let you do the work for me. If you want to follow the program exactly as written, however, feel assured that you will get a gold star on your report card.

Warning: Don't cram too many more miles into this program thinking it will make you a faster runner. It may actually make you a slower runner if you overtrain. A warm-up that is too long on speed days may compromise your ability to run the core part of the workout. I often would do a 2- or 3-mile (3.2-4.8 km) warm-up before a speed session, then a 1- or 2-mile (1.6-3.2 km) cool-down after. Did those extra miles (counted at the end of the week) make me a better runner? Yes and no. Achieving balance in any training program at this level is not easy. If anyone tells you it is easy, walk away from them.

Thursdays

This second day of speed work is what differentiates advanced from intermediate 2. Each Thursday, do a tempo run. Different coaches define this workout differently, but a tempo run in the Higdon songbook is a continuous run, starting slow, with a buildup in the middle to near 10K race pace, then finishing slow. A tempo run of 40 to 60 minutes would begin with 10 to 20 minutes of easy running, build for 20 to 30 minutes near the middle, then finish with 5 to10 minutes easy. The pace buildup should be gradual, not sudden, with peak speed coming about two-thirds into the workout. Jack Daniels suggests peak speed to be the same as the pace you could maintain for 60 minutes. That certainly works for me, although I usually advise runners that peak pace should be somewhat slower than their 10K pace. Yes, that is imprecise; it is meant to be imprecise. Hold that peak only for a few minutes. Five minutes for peak speed sounds about right, but to be honest, I never looked at my watch while doing a tempo run until I got back to the parking lot at Wilson Shelter in Indiana Dunes State Park, where I so frequently ran these workouts.

I consider tempo runs to be the thinking runner's workout. A tempo run can be as hard or easy as you want to make it, and it has nothing to do with how long (in time) you run or how far (in distance). In fact, the times prescribed for tempo runs serve mainly as rough guidelines. Feel free to improvise. Improvisation is at the heart of doing a tempo run correctly.

Fridays

One thing constant in all of my schedules is TGIF: Thank God it's Friday, so Hal gives us a day off. Well, not all runners want to go a day without running. Seven days of running is no problem for them, but I want those of you who are less obsessed to rest so you are better prepared for the weekend long runs. Notice that in the schedule every third Friday offers rest or easy run. Those are weeks with races scheduled on Sunday, so the day of rest gets shifted to Saturdays—and you may want to rest both Friday and Saturday to arrive at the starting line ready to run. If racing on a Saturday, shift the workouts around, either cutting back on the Thursday tempo run or moving it to the postrace Sunday. By the time you get to the advanced level, you should be able to make these minor adjustments without asking my permission.

Saturdays

Some Saturdays feature an easy run, starting at 3 miles (4.8 km), moving upward in the second half of the schedule to 4 miles (6.4 km) or 5 miles (8 km). Other Saturdays, I prescribe pace runs, the pace you plan to run in the half marathon. To succeed in a pace run—hitting that first mile and the miles after as close to half marathon pace as possible—you may want to do a warm-up just as you do before speed sessions. But wait: Think ahead! What kind of warm-up will you be able to achieve in your race, particularly in a race with packed corrals that force you to enter a half hour early or risk getting stuck behind slower runners? Use these Saturday pace runs to rehearse everything that will happen on race day. And maybe that includes launching into race pace without an adequate warm-up.

Sundays

As an experienced runner, you probably already do a long run of 60 to 90 minutes on the weekends. The schedule suggests a slight increase in time as you get closer to race date: from 90 minutes to 1:45 to 2 hours. Don't get hung up on running these workouts too fast. Forget about how many miles you cover. And, yes, you may actually find yourself running farther than 13.1 miles when you run 2 hours. Run at a comfortable, conversational pace, except on those days where a 3/1 run is prescribed.

Let me explain that term. A 3/1 run is one in which you run the first three-fourths of the distance at a comfortable pace, then accelerate to near race pace over the last one quarter of the workout. Notice I said near race pace, not at race pace, or faster than race pace. Pay attention to what the coach says, otherwise you may train yourself into a hole. You should finish refreshed, not fatigued following an all-out sprint. The schedule suggests doing your long runs on Sundays, and while you can do them Saturdays or any other convenient day, you will generally find it easier to run the long runs the day after the pace runs instead of vice versa.

Racing

Most experienced runners enjoy racing, so I've included three races during the training period: one every third week, building from 5K to 10K to 15K. Those particular distances are not magical, and it is not necessary to race. Plug in whatever races look interesting from your local area wherever they fit into your schedule. One benefit: You can use races to test your fitness and predict your finishing time in the half marathon, which allows you to train more intelligently, specifically on days where I prescribe race pace.

Advanced half is not an easy program. It should be difficult, but not oppressive enough that you are bending over gasping for breath after the workouts. That's a no-no. I won't permit it. Keep in mind those two words from Coach Roy Benson I used in the beginning of this chapter: moderately hard! Moderately hard rules the day. That is the way you can ascend to the pinnacle.

13 | Half-Marathoner Walking

Rob Loeffel, 48, 7 feet tall (2.1 m) and a third-grade teacher from Sarasota, Florida, had played basketball for the University of New Mexico, but enjoyed the fact that his wife LeAnne was a runner. (LeAnne Proud Loeffel boasts a half marathon PR of 1:50:19 and also has completed four full marathons.) Rob would have *loved* to match strides with LeAnne, but alas, although he cycled, having completed at least one century (100-mile [161 km] ride), Rob found running difficult to do, saying. "I had jogged some 5Ks in the past, but my knees and body could do no more."

Rob decided that if he could not run, he certainly could walk: "I started walking last summer and decided to attempt the Sarasota Music Half Marathon. I trained for five months and set my goal at 3:30:00, although I just wanted to beat the sag wagon at four hours."

He did better than that, finishing in 3:12:23. "I crushed my goal," says Loeffel, justifiably thrilled by his accomplishment. "That day I was on my own. Everyone was friendly and encouraging. The walkers. The runners. The volunteers."

Meanwhile, LeAnne was amazed by her husband's dedication in training: "For the longest walk, he got up at 2:30 in the morning, went walking, came back and showered, and left to teach his class all day. Incredible!"

Incredible, indeed, LeAnne. Add to the list of The Incredibles, Noelle Dean Brosnan, a property manager from Burlingame, California. For 17 years, Brosnan had done no running or even walking, and her weight had ballooned to 209 pounds (95 kg). A friend sent her one of my half marathon training programs. Brosnan reflects on the 12 weeks she spent focused on her first half. "My goal was just to finish. Anything else was pure bonus. I rocked the half and, changing my eating habits, lost more than 20 pounds (9 kg) in the process." Nevertheless, losing weight was not Brosnan's goal; finishing was. Half marathon walk completed, Brosnan set as one of her next goals, running the same distance.

When I posted information about the Loeffels and Brosnan on Facebook, it attracted the attention of Leona Kay Eaton, 65, a manager from Ashland, Wisconsin. Eaton had run 15 half marathons, but she was thinking more of her husband, who recently had bilateral total knee replacements. After the surgery, he started walking, doing two 5Ks, even some jogging, although his

The 5K Option

During the winter, my wife, Rose, and I enjoy a second home near the ocean outside Jacksonville, Florida. Although I went to college in Minnesota and consider cross-country skiing my favorite cross-training activity, I won't lie to you: I love running at low tide on the beach and riding my bike to coffee shops in January. Plus, there's no need to shovel snow. Rose attends aquarobics classes daily, a couple of dozen women working out in a heated, outdoor pool. Several have become very close friends.

That includes our neighbor, Mary Ellen Reed. A few months before the Gate River Run, Jacksonville's biggest race and a 15K, Rose asked Mary Ellen if she would like to join her in the Gate's companion 5K. "I could never do that," said Mary Ellen. After all, wasn't the Gate a race? Rose pointed out that Mary Ellen frequently walked around her condo or on the beach. "You can do it," Rose insisted, suggesting that 5K was only a mile or so farther than her usual walks.

And so while I was running the Gate's full 15K on a course that crosses two bridges over the St. Johns River, Rose and Mary Ellen walked an out-and-back route into downtown. Mary Ellen and her late husband, Horton, once had lived in the area, so she was able to point out all the churches they passed. The pair finished holding hands. Several days later, Mary Ellen ordered photos, including one that now occupies a proud place on our refrigerator. "It was a breeze," she admitted, "Walking the downtown streets was fun, a new experience."

For spouses who are not runners or even walkers, half marathons often have 5K options, the emphasis more on fitness than on performance, with no winner declared. Everybody ties for first, finishing times irrelevant.

Do you need a special training program to finish a 5K? Probably not. I could write one for you, but the novice running program in chapter 10 will do. Or follow Mary Ellen's lead and walk a few miles daily, and hope you have a friend (or spouse) who talks you into entering a "race" at that distance.

wife worried he might be overdoing it. She laughs: "He covets my half marathon medals and might want one for himself." Leona hoped that my half marathon program for walkers might help her husband achieve that goal.

Easier Than Running?

Walking a half marathon should be easier than running a half marathon, should it not? Not necessarily and for one reason, walkers are out on the course longer than runners. And walkers—God love them—train longer to achieve the same mileage. While the East Africans and fastest of the American men cruise across a half marathon finish line in around 60 minutes, and while most of the runners in the field finish with times under two hours, or at least under three, walkers remain on the course for four. A few take even more time.

More time to suffer from sunburn. More time for blisters to build. More time to suffer heat-related problems. And not all half marathons remain friendly to walkers, sometimes closing the course for those who fail to pass checkpoints within a certain limit. A half marathon I ran recently in Chicago closed its course at 3:30, forcing many to return to the finish line in buses, fair when you consider that the city needs to reclaim its streets for ordinary people at some point, but tough on those walkers and runners who can't maintain a pace somewhere near 15 minutes a mile (9:19/km).

It's okay to take frequent walking breaks when running a half marathon.
Marathonfoto.com

No reliable statistics exist that delineate how many participants in half marathons are runners and how many are walkers and how many are something in between. And how do you classify the many "runners" following one of Jeff Galloway's run/walk programs? Jeff's "Gallowalkers" shift quickly and frequently between running and walking, for instance, alternating 60 seconds of running with 60 seconds of walking. I refuse to draw a line between runners and walkers. Jeff, I've got your back. If we are together in a race, we are all Racers with a capital letter. We are all half-marathoners with the right to slap 13.1 stickers on the back of our SUVs.

Do you need to train differently to walk instead of run a marathon? Not really. At least not that much differently. Pick any of the training programs offered already in this book and write *walk* where I say *run*. These programs will get you there. Nevertheless, enough differences exist between these two styles of locomotion (walk vs. run) that for some years I have provided on my website a slightly different training program for half marathon walkers. But only slightly different.

In many respects, I feel that the half marathon is a much friendlier distance for walkers than the full marathon is. One advantage of a half over a full is that you won't need to spend as much time on the course. Most reasonably fit people should, like Rob Loeffel, be able to walk 13.1 miles in three or four hours. Doing so is fun. It is also exciting to set goals and achieve them. Walking a full marathon is more difficult, less because of the fitness level of the walkers than because of the fact that not all marathons keep their finish lines open for six or seven hours or more. (The Honolulu Marathon is one race that does, by the way.)

My half marathon walking program assumes you currently have the ability to walk for 30 minutes, three or four times a week. That's where the program begins. If that seems difficult, consider going a shorter distance—or take more time to develop an endurance base. Rob Loeffel spent five months getting ready for his half marathon race. (Consider Rob your role model.) Here is my 12-week program for walkers planning to go a half

Farther and Faster

"You'll get some health benefits by going out and walking at any pace, any distance, whenever you can catch time away from your work or other duties," says Mark Fenton. "But all the scientific research proves rather conclusively that you can attain a much higher level of conditioning and well-being if you actually train to improve your aerobic fitness. Every tenth of a liter of aerobic capacity that you can cram into your body by walking farther and faster is going to increase your health and longevity as well" (Higdon 1997b, p. 156).

marathon. (It was designed with the assistance of Mark Fenton, a former competitive racewalker and author of *The Complete Guide to Walking for Health, Weight Loss, and Fitness*.)

First, one caveat: How walker-friendly is the half marathon you choose? Not to be critical, but some half marathon race directors, like full marathon race directors, establish checkpoints that participants must cross by a certain time, otherwise they might be unable to go the full distance, sometimes diverted onto distance-robbing detours, sometimes asked to move from the road to parallel sidewalks, sometimes even (the ultimate embarrassment) forced to climb into a bus for transport to the finish line.

Examples of this are two races that I ran portions of while researching this book. The Indy Mini announces its course completion limit on its website: "The Mini-Marathon has a time limit of 4 hours (18 minutes per mile pace). Participants must be able to maintain the 18 minutes per mile pace or they will be required to board the trail bus." The Rock 'n' Roll Chicago Half Marathon has a slightly faster finish-time limit of 3:30, starting its countdown clock after the last walker or runner passes the starting line. Fail to maintain the stay-in-the-race pace by the 9- and 11-mile markers, and you will be invited to board a bus for a ride back to the finish line.

Once the last walker or runner crosses the starting line, the countdown clock at the Rock 'n' Roll Half in Chicago begins.

Ryan Bethke

That seems unfair and also no fun after all that training, but it is for a sound reason, also explained for Mini participants online: "This limit allows our volunteers to clean and clear the course prior to the streets being open to traffic." Don't blame the race director or the organization or sponsors of the half marathon you want to walk. City management often dictates how long runners (and walkers) may claim the streets as their own. If you don't like a race's policy, please choose a race that leaves the course open longer. The Illinois Marathon and Half Marathon in Champaign, for example, discourages walkers from entering the full marathon, and imposes a time limit of 3:30 for the half marathon, but it does not physically remove walkers, saying, "If you are still on the course after the time limit, you will need to exercise caution as it pertains to automobiles, etc. We will, however, keep the finish line clock running for seven hours from the start of the marathon."

Disclaimer: Illinois race director Jan Seeley serves as my agent and negotiated the contract with Human Kinetics for this book. Jan's policies seem more than reasonable to me and hopefully also to you. Nevertheless, choose carefully the half marathons you plan to walk.

WALKING TRAINING PROGRAM

Week	Mon	Tue	Wed	Thu	Fri	Sat	Sun
1	Rest	30 min easy	20 min stroll	30 min easy	Rest	30 min stroll	3 miles easy
2	Rest	30 min easy	20 min stroll	30 min easy	Rest	30 min stroll	4 miles easy
3	Rest	35 min easy	20 min stroll	35 min easy	Rest	20 min stroll	2 miles brisk
4	Rest	35 min easy	25 min stroll	35 min easy	Rest	25 min stroll	5 miles easy
5	Rest	35 min easy	25 min stroll	35 min easy	Rest	40 min stroll	6 miles easy
6	Rest	40 min easy	25 min stroll	40 min easy	Rest	30 min stroll	4 miles brisk
7	Rest	40 min easy	25 min stroll	40 min easy	Rest	50 min stroll	7 miles easy
8	Rest	40 min easy	25 min stroll	40 min easy	Rest	50 min stroll	8 miles easy
9	Rest	45 min easy	30 min stroll	45 min easy	Rest	30 min stroll	6 miles brisk
10	Rest	45 min easy	30 min stroll	45 min easy	Rest	60 min stroll	9 miles easy
11	Rest	45 min easy	30 min stroll	45 min easy	Rest	60 min stroll	10 miles easy
12	Rest	30 min easy	20 min stroll	30 min stroll	Rest	Rest	Half marathon

Note: To convert English distances to metric, use an online conversion website such as www.onlineconversion.com/length_common.

Once you have chosen your half marathon, the secret to success is consistency. There's that word again, but you need to make walking a regular habit—a daily habit, not just something you do on the weekends or when the weather is nice. Walking coach Mark Fenton states, "The fitness walker must make a positive commitment to exercise a certain number of days a week over a specific distance or length of time, even if some of those days show fairly modest efforts" (Higdon, 1997b, p. 158).

Here's how to begin. The walking program, same as most of my running programs for the half, lasts 12 weeks and begins at a fairly easy level. In week 1, you walk for short amounts of time on three weekdays: Tuesday 30 minutes, Wednesday 20 minutes, and Thursday 30 minutes. (One difference between my running programs and my walking program is that for the former, I prescribe in miles, for the latter in minutes.)

Rest

Rest is important, and because the hardest workouts come on the weekends, I prescribe rest on Mondays, allowing you to recover from the weekend, then I prescribe rest again on Fridays to prepare you for the weekend workouts. If you decide you don't need much rest, particularly early in the program when minutes and miles are low, you won't find me standing on the sidewalk holding a stop sign. As the program nears its end with mileages of 8 (13 km), 9 (14.5 km) and 10 (16 km), you may be happy for these rest days. Incidentally, consider scheduling a massage on Mondays. It will help recovery.

On weekends we do the tough work. One day on the weekend (Saturday), you stroll at an easy pace, *stroll* being a Mark Fenton term, and I'll explain that in the section on pace that follows. The other weekend workout (Sunday) features a prescribed distance, the only workouts defined in miles: 3 miles (4.8 km) in week 1, 4 miles (6.4 km) in week 2, and so on to a maximum of 10 miles (16 km) in week 11, one week before the half marathon. The workouts on the weekend, as well as during the week, get progressively longer, thus more difficult. Because the increases are gradual, you should be able to manage the buildup without excessive strain. Before starting to train, let's consider some of the terms used, all borrowed from racewalker Mark Fenton.

Pace

Don't agonize too much about pace—how fast you walk—at least for the first few weeks. Walk at a stress-free pace. If training with a friend, the two of you should be able to hold a conversation. If you can't talk (and I don't mean talk into a cell phone), you're walking too fast. Mark believes that changing pace can be an effective training tool. You need not walk at the same pace day after day. Following are descriptions of three pace changes from stroll to easy to brisk. While it is easy for Mark and me to put labels on pace changes, inevitably you set your own pace. You determine how fast or slow you need to move to maximize your training without encountering the ogre: overtraining.

Pace	Description	Breathing	How to do it
Stroll	"Window shopping" walking	Normal	Enjoy your walk
Easy	Continuous comfortable walking	Almost normal	Move somewhat faster
Brisk	Walking with real purpose	Harder, but still conversational	Take quicker-than-normal steps

Stroll is the easiest pace. Walk as though you're window shopping at an outlet mall. Easy is just that: easy, but somewhat faster than stroll. Brisk suggests that you pick up the pace, getting just a little out of breath, walking fast enough that you don't notice the sign announcing a sale in the window of the store you just passed. Can you go faster than that? At levels above these three, walkers become power walkers or racewalkers, walking with an elbow-swinging, hip-wiggling form such as that used by those competing in the Olympic Games. You don't want to go that fast, although there are coaches and books to serve anyone who wants to walk at the competitive level.

Distance

This is a time-based program, meaning most of the workouts are prescribed in minutes rather than miles. Forget distance. If you must wear a GPS watch, don't let it force you to go far. Just walk the prescribed length of time and check the readouts later. If you know approximately how fast you walk, you can estimate distance, but during the week, distance is not important. You just want to get out regularly and exercise your legs. Remember the key word used so often in this book: *consistency!*

On Sundays, however, the training schedule does dictate workouts at distances, from 3 to 10 miles (4.8-16 km). Don't worry about walking precisely those distances, but you should come close. Pick a course out your back door or in a scenic area where you think you might enjoy walking and where there are a lot of runners and walkers and cyclists. In deciding where to train, talk to other walkers or runners. They probably can point you to accurately measured courses for your workouts. Where do you find these people? Most cities have specialty running stores that serve walkers as well as runners. By the way, when you visit such a store, get fitted with a comfortable pair of shoes that can serve you both in training and in your ultimate walking event. Be sure to tell the clerk that you are a walker rather than a runner, because it may make a difference in shoe choice.

Long Walks

The most important day of your workout week is Sunday—or the day when you do your long walks. You can flip-flop workouts, by the way, and walk long on any day that is most convenient. The long walks progressively increase in distance two weekends in a row with a third step-back week every third weekend to provide extra relaxation time and a psychological boost. This step-back pattern is one I developed for those using my full marathon programs, and it works well with half marathon walkers, too. Over 12 weeks, your longest walk will increase from 3 to 10 miles. Don't worry about making the final jump from 10 miles in practice to 13.1 miles in the race. Inspiration will carry you to the finish line, particularly if you taper the final week. Notice that week 12, the final week before the half marathon, features reduced mileage, or reduced "minute-age." This will allow you to arrive at the starting line with fresh legs.

Jogging

One way to get to the finish line faster is to do some jogging. If you were a competitive racewalker, you would get disqualified for starting to run, but because you are not competing for a prize, feel free to jog occasionally, either in training or in the half marathon itself. Jog in small segments: 50 to 100 meters every 10 minutes or so might be enough at first. Eventually you might want to expand your jogging segments, or even run the entire way, but don't do too much at first. Running is a more high-impact exercise than walking, so be cautious. Your goal should be to finish the half marathon, not finish it fast.

If you plan to jog and walk in a race that offers prizes in a walking category, you need to enter in the running division. It's unfair to those who walk the whole way for you to be ranked as finishing faster because you ran. If you suddenly become inspired and decide to break into a run a 100 or so yards out from the finish line, be aware that surrounding walkers may not consider that a friendly act. Edging past a walker with your last few strides and raising a fist while shouting, "Yes!" well, that's a no-no.

Take Time

Does the 12-week progression from 3 (4.8 km) to 13.1 miles seem too tough? Do you have more than a dozen weeks before your chosen half? Lengthen the schedule; take 18 or even 24 weeks to prepare. Repeat the week just completed before moving up to the next level. This training schedule is not carved in stone. Feel free to innovate if you feel you need more time to prepare. On the other hand, a lot of thought—both by Mark Fenton and me—went into creating a program offering a path to success. Don't stray too far afield, and you will keep both of us happy.

14 HM₃

I am often asked this question: What is cross-training? Add also other questions flowing out of that first question: Does yoga count as cross-training? What about strength training? Can I play in a soccer game or volleyball match on my cross-training day and still get credit for it? Can I improve my fitness level by cross-training? Will cross-training make me a better runner?

Let's start with the first question: What is cross-training? Because many of my training programs include cross-training, I already have provided my definition, first offered in chapter 10, featuring the novice training programs. To save you the trouble of flipping the pages backward, let me repeat what I wrote: What form of cross-training works best? It could be swimming, cycling, walking, cross-country skiing, snowshoeing. In other words, exercises that are aerobic, meaning they stress your cardiovascular system.

That's pretty simple, but it excludes some of the activities mentioned previously. Yoga as cross-training: No, because as marvelous as this discipline is, yoga is static rather than aerobic. Yoga is not designed to get you out of breath. The same can be said for strength training, although I regularly visit the gym three or more days a week. Great for general fitness, fans, but just not aerobic. As for soccer or volleyball or other sports that involve sideways movements, or even contact, the Mother Hen in me worries that if you continue in those sports during the buildup to a half marathon, you increase your risk of injury, particularly toward the end of one of my progressive training programs when mileage builds and muscle fatigue builds with it. I'll have more to say on that later in the chapter, but the most important question is this: Will cross-training make you a better runner? A qualified "maybe," but there are other reasons why I suggest people cross-train, and let me yield to someone with PhD attached to his name.

Let me introduce you to Richard L. Brown, PhD, a former coach at Athletics West, a coach to Olympic athletes, including Mary Decker Slaney, double gold medalist in the 1983 World Track and Field Championships. In his book, *Fitness Running*, Brown writes "Cross-training is engaging in a physical activity that is not your primary activity" (Brown 2015, p. 117). Brown further suggests that cross-training serves five major purposes:

1. Strengthen and balance muscle groups and their tendons and ligaments
2. Improve or maintain flexibility
3. Provide a mental break from running
4. Substitute other activities for running on easy or rest days
5. Maintain fitness during periods of injury

Yep, Dick Brown got it right, but let me comment further on what he says. In adding cross-training to my programs, I favor the fourth reason when I ask runners to bike or swim or walk or ski. Cross-training becomes a substitute. The third reason, a mental break, is also important; the first and second reasons, improving strength and flexibility, are only slightly less important. But if a single reason stands out from the other four, I

Yoga as Cross-Training

Does yoga count as cross-training? In the strictest sense, no. When I include the word *cross* in one of my training schedules, I mean for runners to do an aerobic activity such as cycling or swimming or walking or cross-country skiing. This offends some yoga devotees, who feel their activity deserves a place at the party. Yoga does, but it still fails to meet the narrow definition I use for cross-training.

That does not mean that yoga is without benefit for runners. Jeremy Berger writes in a *Men's Journal* article, available on the Internet: "Yoga will make you a better runner, improve your form and balance and decrease your susceptibility to overuse injuries." Berger adds that yoga will also improve your focus before and during the race, when mental staying power is as important as physical endurance.

Julie Cowart, 55, an office manager from Stevenson, Washington, incorporates yoga into her training week mainly for its stretching benefits, also for core strengthening: "I love yoga after a run for a great overall stretch. But you do not want to be over zealous. If you become too flexible, it can be bad for the joints." Thus, practice yoga with moderation—including after you cross-train.

would pick the final reason: Maintain fitness during periods of injury. Or what might be a subcategory: Avoid injuries caused by running too much.

If injured, you can maintain, if not improve, fitness by exercising in other sports. In this respect the best exercise is running in deep water while wearing a flotation vest, mimicking the running motions but without impact. Running chest deep in the pool is something I do regularly, but there is some impact. There is little impact in swimming hitting the edge of the pool at the end of each lap, but although I swim frequently, the sport is not a very close match to running. Because of convenience, cycling probably is more popular with recuperating runners, an indoor bike being much safer than an outdoor bike. But cycling may not be an option for certain injuries. This dodges the question somewhat: Will swimming or biking make you a better (i.e., faster) runner. Let me respond with a line from George Gershwin's opera, *Porgy and Bess*: "It ain't necessarily so."

Success in any athletic activity is usually tied to sport-specific training. If you want to become proficient at a sport, you need to focus most of your training on activities that are specific to that sport. Want to be a good basketball player? Running will get you in shape. Strength training will make you stronger. But if you're interested in hitting three-point shots, you need to throw a lot of them up at the backboard. And if you want to be a good runner, you need to focus most of your attention on running.

Running a lot of miles is inevitably what makes you a better runner. Throw some speed work into the mix to fine-tune your performances, to nibble a few seconds (if not minutes) off your personal records. Where does that leave cross-training? Most certainly, cross-training is good for maintaining, if not boosting, aerobic fitness. The main benefit of cross-training

Active Recovery

Eric Smith, 52, an architect from Grayslake, Illinois, started using a stationary recumbent bicycle for cross-training after his wife, Suzanne, asked him to accompany her to the gym in the evenings. "I started using the bike as a time killer while waiting for my wife to complete her workouts."

The recumbent bike proved handy when tendinitis caused by too much mileage forced him to limit his running workouts. Smith most often uses the bike on rest days: "I just figured it would be a good way to cross-train and work the legs in a slightly different way. With an iPod and television at the gym, the time goes fairly fast. I view using a recumbent bike as an active-recovery session."

Smith has run under 1:40 twice for the half marathon and considers a time of 43:00 for the 10K a reasonable goal. More than that, he would like to run 3:30 for the marathon and qualify for Boston. As long as his wife keeps taking him to the gym, those goals should be more than attainable.

is that it allows dedicated runners like me to enjoy life a bit more. It helps us to get out of the rut of running mile after mile day after day. It permits us to relax and exercise by doing something different. As for the very best reason, I'll rest my case with two words: It's fun!

Welcome to HM₃

This leads us to a training program that should please those of you enjoy cross-training for its benefit of being fun. Welcome to half marathon 3, or HM₃ a program similar to my marathon 3 program, which has proved refreshingly popular with runners, often experienced runners, often older runners, who find it stresses their body too much to run four or five or six or even seven days a week. The sigh of relief almost was audible from my Facebook page when I provided dedicated marathoners with a program that featured only three days of running a week. They loved to run, but found that bad things happen if they failed to get sufficient rest between runs. Or at least if they failed to do something different.

Another group that embraced marathon 3 were those boasting backgrounds in sports other than running, particularly the triathlon and its mix of swimming, cycling, and running in a single event. They, too, enjoyed running, but they also enjoyed their other tri sports. And in all honesty, mea culpa, I probably spend more time riding a bike now than I do running. Cross-training makes more sense to my aging body.

Extra Exercises

"I began cross-training while preparing for the Marine Corps Marathon," says Teri Eckel, an underwriter from Rockaway, New Jersey. At age 51, I find that these extra exercises help prevent injury and provide additional strength. I currently mix my strength training routine with about 25 miles (40 km) of running a week. I love the feeling of being stronger, but I'm still not going to give up the cardio workouts, which I love even more."

Before moving on to the HM₃ training program, let me emphasize again why I define cross-training as exercises that are aerobic. *Yoga?* Sorry, great for flexibility, great for the mind, but not aerobic. I do encourage runners to include in their programs yoga, or stretching, or Pilates or even dynamic stretching, such as lunges, but you don't get credit for a cross workout.

Strength training? Same deal. I strongly advise runners to work out in a gym, which I do regularly, but I consider strength training more a supplement to a running program, not part of it. *Soccer?* Love the sport, I was jumping off the couch and screaming while I watched the U.S. women's team win the World Cup, but while I concede that all the running back and forth you do during a soccer match can get you, and keep you, in great shape, you probably want to stay away from sports that require sudden sideways movements as the mileage builds in any of my training program. My ban against sideways sports includes tennis and volleyball. Let me offer again what I said in the earlier chapter.

> Don't make the mistake of cross-training too vigorously. Sports such as basketball or volleyball that involve sideways motions or sudden stops and starts do, in many ways, qualify as cross-training. But realistically, you also may increase your risk of injury if you double up on these sports, particularly as the mileage builds.

As for those other questions offered in the first paragraph of this chapter: Can I improve my fitness level by cross-training? Will cross-training make me a better runner? This results in a conundrum. You will improve fitness, very definitely so. But will you improve as a runner? That's tougher to prove.

Here is where you bump up again to the law of specificity. If you want to become a better runner, you need to train as a runner. You need to run. The more miles you run and the faster you run those miles (within certain limits, of course), the better you become as a runner. *Swimming?* You can improve or maintain your aerobic capacity, but swimming is an upper-body sport; running is a lower-body sport. Gain upper-body weight, more muscle, and it actually will slow you down as a runner. The fastest swimmers in triathlons usually are not the fastest runners, and vice versa.

Bicycling? The fastest cyclists in triathlons also are not always the fastest runners. While you will develop the muscles of the lower leg, often they are the wrong muscles, antagonistic muscles that can slow you if overdeveloped. Have you ever checked the quadriceps muscles of competitors in the Tour de France? Their quads are immense, huge, almost overlapping their kneecaps. It is a wonder that elite cyclists can even walk once they climb off their bikes. The fastest cyclists in triathlons usually are not the fastest runners, and vice versa.

I speak from experience, having passed through what I now call my midlife triathlon crisis. The first triathlon in which I participated was organized by a member of my running club. One year after the first Ironman Triathlon in Hawaii, John Wilson organized a short-distance triathlon on the grounds of La Lumiere School near La Porte, Indiana. It included a swim across a lake of barely 100 yards (91 m), a bike ride of maybe 8 miles (13 km) on rural roads, and a run on the school's cross country course, thus 5K. The event continues to this day as the La Porte County Family YMCA Triathlon, now moved to that city.

My skills as a runner guaranteed early competitive success, and in one triathlon ending on the campus of Purdue University, I finished the 15K

Though cycling is an excellent form of cross-training, it does not develop the right leg muscles to be a strong runner, so it should be used minimally as part of a training program.

running leg with a time only two minutes slower than I had hit in a 15K in Plymouth, Indiana, (the Blueberry Stomp) only two weeks before.

This sport is easy, I thought, deciding that if I trained harder in the other two events, I might achieve greater success. I focused first on cycling, working out sometimes with a local cycling group. Returning two years later to the same triathlon, I knocked more than 10 minutes off my cycling time. Unfortunately, my running leg was that much slower. I felt like I was a character in *Alice's Adventures in Wonderland*. The Red Queen told Alice, "It takes all the running you can do to keep in the same place."

Prescription for Fitness

Thus, why include cross-training in a program aimed at runners if it will not make them faster? It will, but only if done properly, following good training principles. In adding cross-training to my training programs, I do not want to build fitness, or even maintain it. My entire aim is to relax runners before or after the key running workouts. Relax! That is the key word.

Nevertheless, cross-training can offer benefits, one of them being an aerobic buzz. Whether or not it helps you build speed or endurance, cross-training may help you maintain fitness. Running is a high-impact sport. Cross-training thus allows runners to lessen the likelihood of injury by preventing the accumulation of impact forces on bones, tendons, ligaments, and muscles. Although weekly mileage may decrease, you can maintain fitness and enhance recovery after injuries. But which cross-training exercise should you choose?

Cycling? An easy hour's ride on Sunday after a hard 6-miler (9.6 km) on Saturday is perfect. But don't flail away on a thin-tired bike, with your head down not watching the scenery, eyes focused on the computer on your rams-head handlebars, trying to keep the mph readings over 20 (32 kph), racing through stop signs to do so. Instead, behave as I do today. Cruise on your bike for 30 to 60 minutes. My thin-tired bike was consigned long ago to a dumpster. I currently ride a fat-tired bike, sitting straight up, enjoying the scenery, and I don't approach 20 mph, even going downhill.

Swimming? As a triathlete, I usually swam in Lake Michigan parallel to shore, going sometimes a half mile (800 m) or more, before wading ashore to run back along the beach. On only rare occasions did I visit the local YMCA to swim laps. Today, I still swim in Lake Michigan during the summer and use a heated outdoor pool near our condo in Florida during the winter. But, following the advice of exercise scientist David L. Costill, PhD, a top-ranked masters swimmer, I avoid kick turns. Instead, I pause at the end of each lap, catching my breath, clinging to the pool wall, before resuming my cross-pool journey. My goal continues to be relaxation more than increasing fitness, one reason why kick turns seem an unnecessary intrusion. For all its benefits, swimming does a relatively poor job of increasing aerobic capacity. Swimmers tend to have $\dot{V}O_2$max scores much lower than runners, as much as 10 points lower.

Are the low $\dot{V}O_2$max scores for swimmers important? Not really. The sport with the highest $\dot{V}O_2$max scores is cross-country skiing, as much as 10 points in the other direction. Before we started spending our winters in Florida, I loved grabbing my skis and running the half mile to the golf course. All I needed was a few inches of snow to cross-train on skis. I consider Nordic skiing to be the perfect cross-training exercise—but only if you ski in the straight-ahead classic style rather than using the faster skating method. Another great winter option is snowshoeing. Minnesotan Janis Klecker, winner of the 1992 U.S. Olympic Trials marathon, trained frequently on snowshoes made by her husband, Barney, an ultramarathon champion. Janis sometimes even used snowshoes in the summer on grass while recovering from an injury.

Overlooked by many runners, walking also counts as cross-training. And it does not need to be power walking or racewalking. An hour's hike in the woods might be just the dose of gentle exercise you need on a Sunday, recovering from a Saturday long run.

Motivation in the Water

"Usually I do cross-training in a gym," says Dianna Johnson, 48, an addiction therapist from Traverse City, Michigan. "Training for my eighth half marathon (Bayshore), I found it harder and harder to motivate myself to do anything that was not running."

Fortunately for Johnson, the local YMCA had just built a new pool. Having worked out as a swimmer in college, she decided to embrace her old sport once more. Johnson began by swimming 20 laps, taking a break every length. Eventually she worked up to swimming a half mile (800 m), three days a week. "Improved core and upper-body fitness helped get me to the finish line. All those laps in the pool certainly helped my endurance. Plus I have type 1 diabetes, so the swimming coupled with running helps me manage my blood sugar."

Accepting cross-training as an important adjunct to training, how do you blend different aerobic activities into a program that will get you ready for a half marathon? Here is HM_3, a 12-week program that can provide you with a gentle approach to your next 13.1-mile race.

HM₃ TRAINING PROGRAM

Week	Mon	Tue	Wed	Thu	Fri	Sat	Sun
1	Rest	4-mile run	30 min cross	3-mile run	Rest	6-mile run	30 min cross
2	Rest	4-mile run	35 min cross	30 min tempo	Rest	6-mile run	35 min cross
3	Rest	5-mile run	40 min cross	3-mile pace	Rest	7-mile run	40 min cross
4	Rest	5-mile run	45 min cross	4-mile run	Rest	7-mile run	45 min cross
5	Rest	6-mile run	50 min cross	40 min tempo	Rest	8-mile run	50 min cross
6	Rest	4-mile run	30 min cross	3-mile pace	Rest or easy run	Rest	5K race
7	Rest	6-mile run	50 min cross	5-mile run	Rest	9-mile run	50 min cross
8	Rest	6-mile run	50 min cross	50 min tempo	Rest	9-mile run	50 min cross
9	Rest	4-mile run	30 min cross	3-mile pace	Rest or easy run	Rest	10K race
10	Rest	6-mile run	60 min cross	6-mile run	Rest	10-mile run	60 min cross
11	Rest	6-mile run	60 min cross	60 min tempo	Rest	10-mile run	60 min cross
12	Rest	4-mile run	30 min cross	3-mile pace	Rest	Rest	Half marathon

Note: To convert English distances to metric, use an online conversion website such as www.onlineconversion.com/length_common.

HM$_3$ has a definite pattern, and it should be easily recognizable to those of you who have analyzed any of the half marathon training programs already presented in this book. Keeping with the hard/easy philosophy of Bill Bowerman, Tuesday, Thursday, and Saturday are the hard days. Those are the days on which you run. Mondays and Fridays are obvious easy days, and the cross-training workouts on Wednesdays and Sundays probably rate somewhere between.

Week	Mon	Tue	Wed	Thu	Fri	Sat	Sun
1-12	Rest	Run	Cross	Run	Rest	Run	Cross

Please do not make the error of converting those cross-training days into hard days, something that is easy to do, because you will be using somewhat different muscles than you use in running. And that is one of the attractions of cross-training. Because you use muscles not fatigued from your hard running workout the day before, you can train hard on a bike or in the pool. Unfortunately, too much hard training can get you in trouble. Consider the full 12 weeks of the program. You want to reach that 12th week pleasantly fatigued, not totally exhausted. Forget hard/hard. You will have greater success in the half marathon if you master the art of hard/easy.

In addition to the HM$_3$ training pattern just outlined is another HM$_3$ pattern that includes two races leading up to the half marathon. Yes, I expect HM$_3$ to be used more often by experienced runners, veteran runners, perhaps even advanced runners, who can handle frequent racing and who enjoy the race experience.

The two races come in weeks 6 and 9, with the third and final race being the half marathon itself in week 12. Before each race I suggest a minitaper: fewer miles in the Tuesday and Thursday runs than in the weeks before and fewer minutes in the Wednesday taper. I also include an option day on Friday where you can grab an extra day of rest before a Sunday race. If you race on a Saturday, back your rest up another day to rest Thursday and Friday before a Saturday race, and finish the week with cross-training on Sunday. Feel free to improvise to match the local racing scene.

Week	Mon	Tue	Wed	Thu	Fri	Sat	Sun
6	Rest	Fewer miles	Fewer minutes	Fewer miles	Rest or easy run	Rest	Race

The following are additional comments for each of the days of your training week.

Monday

Use Mondays to rest from the weekend and to look forward to the coming week of training. That does not mean you can't stay active—as long as that active is not too active. Monday would be a good day to do strength training. My usual Monday routine while down in Florida where I belong to a fitness center is to spend 5 or 10 minutes in the gym working out on various strength machines. Then I head for the pool to both swim and run in the water. Do you have room in your busy schedule for a similar rest-day workout? Maybe not, but Monday coupled with Wednesday or Thursday is a good day for strength training. Consider also scheduling a massage on one of those days.

Tuesday

This is one of the three running days in HM_3. Compare the numbers between this schedule and my two novice training schedules, and you will discover slightly more miles—but only slightly. A mile here, a mile there, does it really make that much difference? Yes, it does, because if you look at the entire 12 weeks of this or any of my other programs, the miles do add up. In HM_3, we begin with a 4-mile (6.4 km) run in week 1 and ramp upward to 6-mile (9.6 km) runs in weeks 10 and 11, before the last-week taper. Not enough mileage for you? Tuesday is one of the days where you can tack another mile or two to the end of your prescribed workout and achieve more total miles by the end of the program. Small changes can result in large fitness gains.

Wednesday

The two cross-training days are positioned in the middle of the week (Wednesday) and at the end of the weekend (Sunday), allowing maximum distance between them. This is by design. Everything I do in planning a training program is by design. Cross-train on Wednesday, then spend three days in other activities before the next dose of cross-training, then another two days before cross-training in the following week. Makes sense, doesn't it? I prefer to prescribe bouts of cross-training in minutes rather than miles, because you can't compare miles on a bike with miles (or yards) in a pool. Kenneth H. Cooper, MD, did a reasonably good job in crunching numbers for his best-selling series of aerobics books, but it is enough for me to tell you to start with 30 minutes of cross-training in week 1 en route to 60 minutes of the same in week 11. Don't be trapped by numbers. Use them to your advantage.

Thursday

Not every Thursday workout is the same as the Thursday before or the Thursday following. The mileage dosage is 3 miles (4.8 km) in week 1 and

6 miles (9.6 km) by week 10, but the Thursday progression is more subtle than that. Thursdays are like a waltz step: three beats, then repeat. During 12 weeks of Thursdays in HM$_3$, the schedule calls for a run, then a tempo, then pace. Three beats, repeat. Three more beats, repeat. Another three more beats, repeat. Three final beats, and the dance is done. I've explained the difference between runs, tempo runs, and pace runs, but I'll briefly do it again. Run means you run at an easy, conversational pace. A tempo run is one where you begin slowly, accelerate to a pace near your usual 10K pace somewhere in the middle of the workout, then decelerate to your slowest pace. A pace run is simple: You run at the pace you hope to hit in the half marathon.

Friday

In almost all my training schedules, Friday is a rest day. But HM$_3$ in week 6 and again in week 9 offers a dose of racing. If you are going to race, you might as well do it right, and this means taking a two-day minitaper. On Friday, take the day off or jog at most a few miles. On Saturday, do no running. If your chosen race is Saturday rather than Sunday, back up your taper one day. No 5K or 10K on the prescribed weekends? Find a race on a convenient day and at any distance. Don't be trapped by the schedule.

Saturday

Run long, the prescribed distance beginning at 6 miles (9.6 km) in week 1 and climaxing at 10 miles (16 km) in weeks 10 and 11. Is the mileage insufficient to feed your inner beast? If you are used to doing longer runs and can run those extra miles comfortably, feel free to add a mile here, two or three miles there. My half marathon training programs for advanced runners peak at 16 miles (26 km), and all my marathon programs peak at 20 (32 km). Unlike training for a marathon, where running farther than the final 26.2-mile distance is not a great idea, you can get away with long runs past 13.1 miles without excessive fatigue while training for races of that distance.

Sunday

Sunday calls for more cross-training. While I am happy with any cross-training exercise you choose, gosh, Sunday is a great day for a bike ride—unless it is January and you live in the frozen north. Like Wednesday, the prescription is in minutes, not miles, beginning with 30 minutes in week 1, peaking at 60 minutes in weeks 10 and 11. Want to do more than an hour cross-training workout on the weekend? Might be a good idea; might not. Sunday ends the workout week, and you begin again on Monday.

Is HM$_3$ with its blend of running and cross-training the perfect training program for you? Two types of runners might benefit most from this program: 1) Those runners who are experienced and (can I say?) aging individuals who find that 4, 5, 6 or even 7 days of run training no longer works for them, yet they still want to stay fit and compete in half marathons; and 2) those who love to run, but also love to bike and swim and participate in other cross-training activities. Call this group tri-based runners if you want. HM$_3$ promises to offer those in either of those groups a new approach to their training. If that is you, I know you will enjoy HM$_3$.

15 | Tween

How many races are enough? How many are too many? Those are questions that each runner must answer, disregarding what the so-called gurus of our sport, and fellow runners quoting those gurus, say. Different people have different answers. A first-timer who has stretched to achieve a half marathon goal may need more recovery time than an experienced runner with dozens of races (many of them half marathons) on his or her résumé. Run 50 or more miles (80 km) a week 50 or more weeks of the year and, yes, you can hippety-hop from race to race, cherry-picking, choosing the ones that are most fun. Although I concede that even experienced runners often overtrain and overrace themselves into injuries.

Consider that if you routinely follow one of my 12-week training programs, you probably can only fit four half marathons (4 × 12 = 48 weeks, plus 4 weeks off) into a year. And if one of those races is a full-distance marathon with 18 weeks of preparation, your racing schedule may become slimmer still.

Or you can embrace the half marathon with all its glories, a 13.1-miler here, a 13.1-miler there, the hippety-hop approach suggested earlier. Is a 12-week buildup necessary for every half marathon? Nahhh. Not if you are willing to accept the fact that playing the "race card" too often may limit your opportunity to achieve a peak performance, a personal record (PR). Half marathons can be *run* rather than *raced*, embraced as 13.1-mile workouts shoulder to shoulder with likeminded friends.

Are you a tween? I'm going to steal that term and apply it to my most foolish friends who want to race frequently. If you are someone with finish-line photos on the wall and a closet full of bling, how do you define success? What do you do between half marathon races? How should you train if you have two months or less between one half marathon and the next—or between one half marathon and a race at any distance, even a full marathon?

For some time I have offered what are labeled multiple marathon programs on my website and also have provided matching interactive programs for two, three, four, five, six, seven, and eight weeks between full marathons. But up until now, there have been no similar programs for half-marathoners, nothing in the way of a multiple half marathon program to guide runners who race that distance frequently. Partly it was because of my attitude. Half marathons are easy, I reasoned. They don't beat you up as badly as full marathons. You don't need me holding your hand if you are a tween. I concede now that I might be wrong.

True, you probably do not need to back all the way down to week 1 each time you set your sights on a half. After a reasonable amount of time for rest and recovery, you can begin in the middle. Experienced runners know that. They know that after several weeks' recovery, they can move on to the next half marathon with less than a 12-week window for training. This is particularly true if the half just finished was run at less than best effort, at fun run pace just to enjoy the experience. A 13.1-mile run thus becomes an extralong workout.

One More Time

Conventional wisdom suggests that you do no more than one, at the most two, marathons a year. The elite runners who win big prize money at Boston, Chicago, or New York rarely run more than that, because to win, or even run a PR, you need to focus intently on a single goal for much longer than the 12 or 18 weeks I prescribe in most of my training plans.

But for half marathons, it's Welcome to happy time! Yes, you can run more than one or two halfs a year. One a month? One each week? I'm not going to suggest a numerical limit. I do know that the runners highlighted in the following examples enjoyed their multiple half marathons.

Katherine Barski: This past fall and winter, I raced a half marathon every other week, for several months. Once you get up to mileage to complete the event, the races themselves allow you to maintain fitness. On the off weeks, I would do an 8-miler (13 km) or a 10-miler (16 km). You can't race all of them hard, of course, so some halfs need to be just fun, easy races.

Penny Buchman: I ran my first half of the season in March, then jumped into others that seemed like fun throughout the spring and summer until my fall marathon. I kept my long runs between 12 and 15 miles (19-24 km), and midweek runs between 3 and 7 (4.8-11.2 km), with one rest day and one cross-training day. During this tween time, if my body asked for an extra rest day or two, I listened.

Kirsten Screen: I just kept my long runs above 12 miles (19 km), with tempo runs and speed training of 3 to 6 miles (4.8-9.6 km) twice midweek. Lifting, yoga, and one hour-long full-body stretching sessions made up the rest of my week. I add more rest days as needed.

Riannon McCord: Last year I ran a half on the Fourth of July, then another three weeks later. I kept my weekly mileage the same and focused mostly on increasing my long runs: a progression from 7 to 8 to 9 miles (11.2, 13, 14.5 km), or something like that. Sometimes I ran the higher end of long-run mileage, but sometimes lower end, depending on how much recovery my legs felt like they needed.

Ellen Boettrich: For two halfs four weeks apart, I held long-run mileage at 8 or 9 miles (13-14.5 km) between. For a half four weeks after a full, I used the half as part of my post-marathon recovery, where I did long runs of 5, 8, and 10 miles (8, 13, 16 km) the weeks between. During the middle of the week, I tossed in a couple of short and fast runs on Tuesdays and Thursdays (hills, tempo, intervals) with an easy run of 4 to 6 miles (6.4-9.6 km) between.

Asha Kumar: I ran half marathons in September, December, and March. I used your beginner plan for the September race, then just went back to week 5 and redid the same plan for the next race in December. I did the same between December and March. Feeling ready for some speed work, I moved up to an intermediate plan for June, then started back at week 7 for a postrace half marathon in October.

Shane Lennon: I did seven half marathons last year between April and September with varying degrees of success. I suffered from bad shin splints, which at times left me unable to train. Big mistake, but I learned to respect the distance and be realistic with my goals.

Karlin Helms Warner: I did two a month apart last year. I ran easy for the first week after the first half, then repeated the last few weeks of my training plan, then a final taper into the second half. Worked like a charm: PRs both times.

Liz Badley: I love the half marathon distance because you can recover quickly enough to run a lot of them. I do two to five each spring (with some 10-milers [16 km] in there, too), using some races as training runs to get ready for my goal race.

What I love about these comments is that everybody trained between their multiple half marathons just a little bit differently, yet while maintaining the basic pattern that had led them into their initial half marathon race.

Training Strategies

To run multiple half marathons without raising your risk of injury, you need to know what you're doing. Here are some training strategies:

1. **Plan your schedule early.** Select your next half marathon, or other long-distance races, well in advance. That allows you to plan your training around more than one event.

2. **Don't ignore rest.** Your body needs time to rebound before training hard again. Muscle soreness ends after a few days, but full recovery may take longer.

3. **Try shorter events.** Races at 5K, 10K, and other distances less than the half marathon still are worthy of your attention. Think of them as speed work.

4. **Don't run all half marathons hard**. Enter some seeking less than peak performance. This makes the most sense if running back-to-back half marathons with less than eight weeks between.

5. **Take time to prepare.** When serious about a half marathon, prepare carefully. Use the full 12 weeks of one of my programs to ensure a personal best.

Here are training strategies for runners running half marathons two, four, six, and eight weeks apart. If you're running half marathons with an odd number of weeks between, simply repeat one of the middle weeks.

TWO WEEKS BETWEEN

Week	Mon	Tue	Wed	Thu	Fri	Sat	Sun
1	Rest	Rest	2-mile run	2-mile run	Rest	60 min run	60 min cross
2	Rest	3-mile run	4-mile run	3-mile run	Rest or run	Rest	Half marathon

Note: To convert English distances to metric, use an online conversion website such as www.onlineconversion.com/length_common.

With only two weeks between half marathons, you really don't have time to train. Focus instead on recovery. Maintain the same high-carbohydrate diet between races that you (hopefully) did before the first. Schedule a massage 48 to 72 hours after the first half and (if your budget permits) a second (gentle) massage before the second.

You may want to do as much walking as running in the workouts just outlined. On Saturday, I suggest a run of about an hour. I don't care how far you run, and I certainly don't want you to run fast. And the cross-training on Sunday is 60 more minutes. An hour of cycling, swimming, or walking with stretching and strength training this day will help with recovery. You can even cross-train on one or two of the midweek days. Regardless of what you do during these two weeks, you are not going to improve your fitness. So concentrate instead on easy activities that will promote your recovery.

FOUR WEEKS BETWEEN

Week	Mon	Tue	Wed	Thu	Fri	Sat	Sun
1	Rest	Rest	2-mile run	2-mile run	Rest	60 min run	60 min cross
2	Rest	3-mile run	4-mile run	3-mile run	Rest	60 min run	60 min cross
3	Rest	3-mile run	5-mile run	3-mile run	Rest	60 min run	60 min cross
4	Rest	3-mile run	4-mile run	3-mile run	Rest or run	Rest	Half marathon

Note: To convert English distances to metric, use an online conversion website such as www.onlineconversion.com/length_common.

With four weeks between marathons, you have the opportunity to at least do some training. It will be more for your mind than for your body. Physically, your body should still be in recovery mode, but I know from my own experiences running too many races in too short a time that successful running is as much psychological as it is physical. So do some training; just don't overdo it.

In the four-week training program outlined, the first week should be entirely for recovery (and don't overlook what I said earlier about the benefits of massage).

The fourth week is your taper week. The two weeks between provide time for training. I have prescribed the weekend workouts in hours rather than miles to allow flexibility. If you are an intermediate or advanced runner who is accustomed to doing speed work, you might want to pick Tuesdays or Thursdays or both for fast running. But please don't overdo it. What kind of speed work? The same kind you were doing leading into the half marathon. Don't experiment with anything new.

SIX WEEKS BETWEEN

Week	Mon	Tue	Wed	Thu	Fri	Sat	Sun
1	Rest	Rest	2-mile run	2-mile run	Rest	60 min run	60 min cross
2	Rest	3-mile run	4-mile run	3-mile run	Rest	75 min run	60 min cross
3	Rest	3-mile run	5-mile run	3-mile run	Rest	75 min run	60 min cross
4	Rest	3-mile run	6-mile run	3-mile run	Rest	90 min run	60 min cross
5	Rest	3-mile run	5-mile run	3-mile run	Rest	90 min run	60 min cross
6	Rest	2-mile run	4-mile run	2-mile run	Rest or run	Rest	Half marathon

Note: To convert English distances to metric, use an online conversion website such as www.onlineconversion.com/length_common.

Six weeks between marathons offers more time for recovery and tapering—but also more time for training. Thus the conundrum: On what element should you focus during this period between marathons? I can't answer that question. You will need to read your own body signals.

I am inclined to suggest that you continue to think recovery the first week after the first half marathon and think taper one week before the next half marathon. That allows you four weeks of what might be described as serious training. That could include speed work as suggested when you have four weeks between. But be cautious about pressing too hard on the accelerator pedal. And don't be afraid to program in more rest days, if necessary. I continue to recommend massages.

EIGHT WEEKS BETWEEN

Week	Mon	Tue	Wed	Thu	Fri	Sat	Sun
1	Rest	Rest	2-mile run	2-mile run	Rest	60 min run	60 min cross
2	Rest	3-mile run	4-mile run	3-mile run	Rest	75 min run	60 min cross
3	Rest	3-mile run	5-mile run	3-mile run	Rest	75 min run	60 min cross
4	Rest	3-mile run	6-mile run	3-mile run	Rest	90 min run	60 min cross
5	Rest	3-mile run	6-mile run	3-mile run	Rest	90 min run	60 min cross
6	Rest	3-mile run	6-mile run	3-mile run	Rest	90 min run	60 min cross
7	Rest	3-mile run	6-mile run	3-mile run	Rest	60 min run	60 min cross
8	Rest	3-mile run	4-mile run	2-mile run	Rest or run	Rest	Half marathon

Note: To convert English distances to metric, use an online conversion website such as www.onlineconversion.com/length_common.

With eight weeks between half marathons, you have time to do serious training. One option certainly would be to revisit the half marathon training program leading up to your recently completed race, and after an easy week 1, use the final seven weeks (weeks 6 through 12) of that program. As with the previous programs, consider that the first week is for recovery and the last week is for tapering.

I'm not sure you need a lot of extra mileage. If you feel fully recovered, run some of the 6-milers (9.6 km) on Wednesday at an up-tempo, even practicing race pace for some, if not all, of those workouts. Advanced runners can do speed workouts, but be cautious about running to exhaustion. I would concentrate more on quality than quantity at this point.

Will one of these programs get you through your second half marathon or third or fourth or more? As runners, we learn as we go. But what if instead of a second half marathon, you decide on a full marathon? Gulp!

To the Marathon and Beyond

Many runners following my 18-week training programs run a half marathon en route to a full marathon. I prescribe a half in week 8 for novice runners or in week 9 for intermediate and advanced runners. But what if you finish a half marathon, particularly a first half marathon, and a lightbulb goes off over your head at 3:00 in the morning the day after your race. (Despite fatigue, you're sleeping fitfully because your mind is full of the joy of your accomplishment while, ouch, your muscles hurt.) Some runners probably complete their half marathon, enjoy the experience, and think "Hey, I'm halfway to a full marathon. I think I'll keep going and do one of those, too."

Well, they can. Actually, they are more than halfway there when you consider that in their half marathon, they just ran 13.1 miles, which puts them only 7 miles (11.2 km) (actually 6.9 miles) away from the 20-miler that serves as the longest run in all my marathon training programs. Please notice that I am using the pronoun they rather than you. I don't want to push you into a marathon too soon after a just-completed half.

Nevertheless, the lure of more bling is tempting. But at what point do you take two steps sideways and shift from the half marathon just completed to one of my marathon programs that will allow you to put a 26.2 sticker on the back of your car opposite the 13.1 sticker just purchased at the expo? It depends a lot on which marathon you want to run. If you want to run Chicago or Marine Corps or New York City, you probably can't get in because they filled up months before that lightbulb went off. For most other full marathons, yes, it is easy to file your entry online and show up at the starting line in another 8 or 10 or 12 weeks after your just-completed half. It is also easy to decide how to train because you have this book in hand. You simply count 8 weeks or 10 weeks or 12 weeks back from the date of your just-identified goal marathon, and that is where you begin.

If you do not yet have a goal marathon, you need to pick one, and one factor in deciding which 26.2-mile race to run is how you can maximize training. Let's use the novice 2 half marathon program and examine the last two weeks.

Week	Mon	Tue	Wed	Thu	Fri	Sat	Sun
11	Rest	3-mile run	5-mile run	3-mile run	Rest	12-mile run	60 min cross
12	Rest	3-mile run	2-mile pace	3-mile run	Rest	Rest	Half marathon

Next, compare those two weeks leading into your half marathon and compare them to weeks 8 and 9 of my novice 2 program for the full marathon, the weeks leading into the test half marathon race prescribed for those using my 18-week program to prepare for a full marathon.

Week	Mon	Tue	Wed	Thu	Fri	Sat	Sun
8	Rest	4-mile run	7-mile run	4-mile run	Rest	15-mile run	60 min cross
9	Rest	4-mile run	7-mile pace	4-mile run	Rest	Rest	Half marathon

Not a perfect match, but close. The difference is a gap of a few miles in the midweek workouts and a gap of a few miles more in the weekend long runs. It comes down to 15 miles vs. 12 miles (24 vs. 19 km) the weekend before the half, a 3-mile (4.8 km) gap. Realistically speaking, you are not that far off, particularly because those finishing their half marathon training and those in the middle of their full marathon ended their second weeks running 13.1 miles. If you crossed that finish line exhilarated instead of exhausted, you may be ready to move up to the longer distance.

Examine the novice 2 marathon program that follows, and you will see that I have merged the final two weeks of your half marathon training with the two weeks leading up to the half marathon in my novice 2 marathon program. You're going to need recovery time after that half, but luckily, week 9 in the novice 2 marathon program is a step-back week, most significantly with only an 11-miler (17.7 km) on the weekend. Only? Would you have thought you might be saying "only 11 miles" when you did your week 1 long run, which was a prodigious 4 miles (6.4 km)? Things change. And you are now a fitter you.

To bridge the gap, I've nibbled away at the midweek mileage in your new marathon program. An extra day of rest on Tuesday. A 5-mile (8 km) run instead of a 7-mile (7.2 km) run on Wednesday. Thursday? Two miles (3.2 km) should be enough. Rest on Friday. Can you comfortably cover 11 miles (17.7 km) on Saturday? If not, maybe doing a marathon in another couple of months is not that bright an idea. If you think an extra easy day might help, shift the 11-miler to Sunday. After that, you are following the track of novice 2 marathon training. The "minus" weeks refer to 2 weeks and 1 week before the half marathon. Once past the half, you merge with my regular full marathon program.

This program is novice 2. What if you come to that just-crossed half marathon finish line from another level of training? If from novice 1, maybe you need more time before moving up from the half to full marathon. If from any of the intermediate or advanced programs, the switch follows the same principles. Put the intermediate or advanced half marathon and full marathon programs together, and simply manipulate some of the numbers. If you don't know how to do this, the do-it-yourself programs in the next chapter should help.

Novice 2 Marathon Program

Week	Mon	Tue	Wed	Thu	Fri	Sat	Sun
-2	Rest	3-mile run	5-mile run	3-mile run	Rest	12-mile run	60 min cross
-1	Rest	3-mile run	2-mile pace	2-mile run	Rest	Rest	Half marathon
9	Rest	Rest	5-mile run	2-mile run	Rest	11-mile run	60 min cross
10	Rest	4-mile run	8-mile pace	4-mile run	Rest	17-mile run	60 min cross
11	Rest	5-mile run	8-mile run	5-mile run	Rest	18-mile run	60 min cross
12	Rest	5-mile run	8-mile pace	5-mile run	Rest	13-mile run	60 min cross
13	Rest	5-mile run	5-mile pace	5-mile run	Rest	19-mile run	60 min cross
14	Rest	5-mile run	8-mile run	5-mile run	Rest	12-mile run	60 min cross
15	Rest	5-mile run	5-mile pace	5-mile run	Rest	20-mile run	60 min cross
16	Rest	5-mile run	4-mile pace	5-mile run	Rest	12-mile run	60 min cross
17	Rest	4-mile run	3-mile run	4-mile run	Rest	8-mile run	60 min cross
18	Rest	3-mile run	2-mile run	Rest	Rest	2-mile run	Marathon

Note: To convert English distances to metric, use an online conversion website such as www.onlineconversion.com/length_common.

16 | Do-It-Yourself Training

Luc Crombez had a question related to the sequence of the training runs. A Belgian expatriate living in Hungary, Crombez, age 55, contacted me by e-mail saying that he was running five days a week totaling about 45 or 55 kilometers a week. (That's 28 to 34 miles a week for those of you challenged metrically). Here is one of Luc's typical weeks:

Monday: Fartlek

Tuesday: 5K recovery

Wednesday: 9K (5.6 miles) tempo run

Thursday: Rest

Friday: Long run, 18K to 22K (11-13.7 miles)

Saturday: Recovery 5K

Sunday: Rest or cross-train

Okay. Not exactly one of my training programs, but close. More important than what he was doing—the numbers in the boxes—was that he wanted to do something slightly different, and he came to me, his online coach, for advice. I didn't know I was Luc's online coach until I got his message, but that's how it works in my corner of cyberspace.

He runs his long runs on Fridays for convenience, but wondered whether there was a reason in the intermediate 1 marathon program he had been loosely following for the weekend combination: Saturday pace, Sunday long.

Yes, there is, and those of you who have been paying close attention so far in this book probably already know the answer, which I'll get to soon. Meanwhile, here's the altered program that Luc proposed:

Monday: Pacing (was the Hal Higdon Saturday run)

Tuesday: Recovery (your Tuesday run, unchanged)

Wednesday: Midweek long run (your Wednesday run, unchanged)

Thursday: Rest (your Friday rest day)

Friday: Long run (your Sunday long run)

Saturday: Recovery (your Thursday run)

Sunday: Cross-train (moved from Monday)

"Is this okay?" Luc Crombez nervously asked, "or would it be better to have the pace and long run closer together, then move the Wednesday midweek run to Monday?" Here is my brief response: "Yes there is a reason for the pace/long weekend combination, but you can modify my programs to suit yourself. I usually like runners to go into the pace runs fresh as they would in a race. Then go into the long run a little tired so they can resist the temptation to run too fast."

Luc responded quickly over the thousands of miles that separated us, "So basically, I could do the pace run on Monday as I come out of the weekend rested. I could still switch the Monday pace run with the Wednesday sorta-long run, if you think that is better."

Rocket Science Running

Writing in *The Runner's Edge,* coauthors Stephen J. McGregor, PhD, and Matt Fitzgerald suggest that runners can minimize the need for spontaneous training reductions by training appropriately. Well, okay: Who can argue with that statement?

"Don't ramp up your training workload too quickly," they write. "Don't try to do more than three hard workouts a week, follow each hard day with an easy day (featuring an easy run, an easy cross-training workout, or complete rest), and plan reduced workload recovery weeks into your training every few weeks" (McGregor and Fitzgerald 2010, p. 91).

In other words, it's not rocket science, folks. Despite the many science-based training programs available in *The Runner's Edge,* there's no substitute for a runner (or coach) who knows (despite the training program being followed) when it is time to run hard and time to run easy and time to rest. "At these times," say the coauthors, "it's important that you listen to your body and reduce your training for a day or two or three to put your body back on track" (McGregor and Fitzgerald 2010, p. 91). Or back on the roads.

It was mainly a cop-out on my part, but I suggested he could do either. I was comfortable with his revision of my training programs. This is as true in real life as in running, but sometimes you need to move out from the shadow of your teacher and use his or her advice to move beyond what was taught. My wife, who was an elementary school teacher, would tell you that this is the greatest compliment you can offer any teacher: to learn from what you have been taught and to move into a new dimension. Which brings us (thank you, Luc) do the do-it-yourself chapter as we come to the end of *Hal Higdon's Half Marathon Training*.

Designed for Success

How do you design a training program to ensure success in a half marathon? How do you choose the workouts that will result in not only a fast finish but also an enjoyable experience in this signature race? More to the point, how did I, the author, create the programs that fill the pages of this book? Programs for fast runners. Programs for slow runners. Programs for a lot of people in between. Programs for old runners. Programs for young runners. Programs for male runners. Programs for female runners, although both sexes seem to train alike. Programs for new runners. Programs for experienced runners. Programs for novice, intermediate, and advanced

Nothing beats developing your own half marathon training plan, following it, and then finishing your race and knowing that all your hard work was worth it.
Courtesy of 500 Festival.

runners. Programs for people who understand the scientific theories that are at the base of endurance training and programs for people who do not.

It is easier than you think. Before I release you to train on your own, let me offer this do-it-yourself training program. Hear first what Russell R. Pate, PhD, professor of exercise science at the University of South Carolina has to say. Dr. Pate, a past president of the American College of Sports Medicine, possesses a marathon best of 2:15:20, having run that fast while placing seventh at Boston in 1975. I quote Russ frequently, but more than that, he is the guardian angel hovering over my shoulder when I design programs such as those in this book. I often would ask myself: What would Russ do?

This takes me back to previous conversations with Russ, with one exchange that underlines perfectly how to design effective training programs. Dr. Pate suggested that runners figure out the key sessions they need for their program. "Get them in there, then surround them with those kinds of recovery activities that allow them to continue over a period of time," he suggests. "Build their programs on priorities." Dr. Pate identifies the key hard sessions as possessing the highest priorities.

Comparing Dr. Pate's recommendations with my novice 2 half marathon training program, the key workout is the weekly long run, Saturday in that program. Second in importance would be the Wednesday run with slightly more mileage than on the Tuesday and Thursday runs bracketing it, and some of those runs feature race pace. Looking at my toughest half marathon training program, advanced, in addition to back-to-back runs on weekends, the two speed workouts on Tuesdays and Thursdays are important for runners at that level.

Do you want to achieve success as a half marathoner? Dr. Pate would advise that it is not what type of workouts you do, whether high or low intensity, but how those workouts are structured into a specific program and incorporated throughout a training year—and for the length of a career as well.

Reread those three paragraphs. Think about what Russ told me. Keep those comments in mind as we move forward into designing a Russ Pate–inspired do-it-yourself training program. For the half marathon, the long run certainly is the key session for runners at all levels. Which other sessions might also be considered key would vary from runner to runner, based on both talent and experience.

Let's shift from exercise science briefly to computer science. When I design a program, I begin by using Microsoft Word to create a table: 7 boxes across, one for each day of the week; 12 boxes down, one for each week if it is a 12-week half marathon program. Add to that a row across the top for the days of the week and a column down the left side where I can number each week. On my computer, I click first on the *insert* tab in the tool bar, then click on *table*, and specify 8 × 13. Here is that table with the days of the week and the number of weeks already added. Also added is the goal race on Sunday of the 12th week, although the race also could be on a Saturday.

Moving forward, let's construct a training program, in this case borrowing the advanced half marathon program, chosen because it is more interesting than my novice and intermediate programs, and because it offers more toys with which to play. Remember what Russ Pate said about figuring out the key sessions needed for the program. "Get them in there," was his command.

Week	Mon	Tue	Wed	Thu	Fri	Sat	Sun
1							
2							
3							
4							
5							
6							
7							
8							
9							
10							
11							
12							Half marathon

If I were in a classroom, or even on Facebook, and asked, "What is the key session in training for a half or full marathon," all the hands would go up, and the answer would come rocketing back to me: "The long run!"

Yep: got it right! Smart class. For most runners with real lives, long runs are best done on the weekends, when they have time to run two or three or four or more hours without the pressure of going to work. All my training programs are front-loaded on Saturdays and Sundays. Novice runners run long on Saturdays; intermediate and advanced runners run long on Sundays. Let's start filling the empty boxes in our matrix. Your computer skills should be more than enough. Type "Long run" into the box for the first Sunday, then copy and paste it all the way down through week 11. (Week 12, of course, features the half marathon.) Don't worry about how long the long run will be. We'll make that decision later.

Week	Mon	Tue	Wed	Thu	Fri	Sat	Sun
1							Long run
2							Long run
3							Long run
4							Long run
5							Long run
6							Long run
7							Long run
8							Long run
9							Long run
10							Long run
11							Long run
12							Half marathon

That fills one column, six to go. With Russ Pate still looking over our shoulders, what workouts do we choose next? Russ said the key sessions, didn't he? *Plural.* Let's add speed work on two days of the week: Tuesdays and Thursdays, those days chosen because we want to allow air between the three most important sessions. Here are examples of speed work we could use:

Hill Training

Hills develop the quadriceps muscles, whether you are training for a hilly race or not. Pick a short hill that is not too steep. Run it multiple times, jogging between repeats for recovery.

Interval Training

This workout is best done on a 400-meter track. A single fast lap around that track would be called a repeat, or repetition, or simply rep. Run that distance or other short distances multiple times, jogging or walking between each rep (the actual interval) for recovery.

Tempo Runs

Different coaches define tempo runs different ways. A Hal Higdon tempo run starts easy and features a gradual buildup to near 10K race pace about halfway into the workout. Hold for a few minutes, then gradually slow to an easy pace.

Other forms of speed work are repeats, fartlek, sprints, strides. If I were designing a program for 5K or 10K, I might use them, but this is a program for half-marathoners. We'll stick with the three basic speed workouts I described as we copy and paste.

We already chose Tuesday as one of the speed-work days. I'm going to prescribe both hill training and interval training for Tuesdays, alternating from one to the other for the first six weeks (three hill sessions), then switch to interval training exclusively for the final six weeks of the 12-week program. I won't assign frequency of the reps yet, saving that for later.

Thursday is the other speed work day, saved exclusively for tempo runs. I absolutely love tempo runs. They are my favorite workout because the runner is not trapped into seconds and minutes ticking away on his watch as is true with hill and track repeats. The runner ignores his or her watch during a tempo run, accepting a speed dictated by perceived exertion alone. Are you tired from your workouts Tuesday and Wednesday? You can trim the sails on Thursday. Or the opposite is also true. If you are exhilarated after the two previous days, let it rip! You determine the effort level, not some Internet-based coach. Here's the filled-in chart for the speed workouts:

Week	Mon	Tue	Wed	Thu	Fri	Sat	Sun
1		Hill repeats		Tempo run			Long run
2		Interval training		Tempo run			Long run
3		Hill repeats		Tempo run			Long run
4		Interval training		Tempo run			Long run
5		Hill repeats		Tempo run			Long run
6		Interval training		Tempo run			Long run
7		Interval training		Tempo run			Long run
8		Interval training		Tempo run			Long run
9		Interval training		Tempo run			Long run
10		Interval training		Tempo run			Long run
11		Interval training		Tempo run			Long run
12		Interval training		Tempo run			Half marathon

We have three columns filled with hard days. What did Russ Pate suggest for the other days of the week? He suggested we surround them with those kinds of recovery activities that allow you to maintain consistent training for weeks and months and even years.

That suggests three to four easy days, but let's start with two of those days. Monday is the day after the long run. Novice runners using my half marathon programs have a day of rest. Intermediate runners cross-train. Advanced runners don't get a day off. No mercy. I offer them the opportunity to rest or run on Monday, but not run too hard. Wednesday is another day for easy runs between the two speed work sessions. Friday? Time for a day off before the weekend, although I recognize that not all advanced runners welcome a day off.

Week	Mon	Tue	Wed	Thu	Fri	Sat	Sun
1	Easy run	Hill repeats	Easy run	Tempo run	Rest		Long run
2	Easy run	Interval training	Easy run	Tempo run	Rest		Long run
3	Easy run	Hill repeats	Easy run	Tempo run	Rest		Long run
4	Easy run	Interval training	Easy run	Tempo run	Rest		Long run
5	Easy run	Hill repeats	Easy run	Tempo run	Rest		Long run
6	Easy run	Interval training	Easy run	Tempo run	Rest		Long run
7	Easy run	Interval training	Easy run	Tempo run	Rest		Long run
8	Easy run	Interval training	Easy run	Tempo run	Rest		Long run
9	Easy run	Interval training	Easy run	Tempo run	Rest		Long run
10	Easy run	Interval training	Easy run	Tempo run	Rest		Long run
11	Easy run	Interval training	Easy run	Tempo run	Rest		Long run
12	Easy run	Interval training	Easy run	Tempo run	Rest		Half marathon

One day remains to be filled, and I am going to fill Saturday with a run that fits somewhere between hard and easy. For the time being, let's refer to the Saturday runs as *medium runs*. This refers to a workout that is not quite as hard as the hard workouts and not quite as easy as the easy workouts. It's somewhere in between. Stated another way, our 12-week program, thus, features three and a half hard workouts, the key sessions that Russ Pate talked about earlier.

Week	Mon	Tue	Wed	Thu	Fri	Sat	Sun
1	Easy run	Hill repeats	Easy run	Tempo run	Rest	Medium run	Long run
2	Easy run	Interval training	Easy run	Tempo run	Rest	Medium run	Long run
3	Easy run	Hill repeats	Easy run	Tempo run	Rest	Medium run	Long run
4	Easy run	Interval training	Easy run	Tempo run	Rest	Medium run	Long run
5	Easy run	Hill repeats	Easy run	Tempo run	Rest	Medium run	Long run
6	Easy run	Interval training	Easy run	Tempo run	Rest	Medium run	Long run
7	Easy run	Interval training	Easy run	Tempo run	Rest	Medium run	Long run
8	Easy run	Interval training	Easy run	Tempo run	Rest	Medium run	Long run
9	Easy run	Interval training	Easy run	Tempo run	Rest	Medium run	Long run
10	Easy run	Interval training	Easy run	Tempo run	Rest	Medium run	Long run
11	Easy run	Interval training	Easy run	Tempo run	Rest	Medium run	Long run
12	Easy run	Interval training	Easy run	Tempo run	Rest	Medium run	Half marathon

All the boxes in the matrix now have been filled, but details remain to be decided: How long is the long run? How short are the easy runs? And what about all that speed work? How many hill repeats? How many reps for the interval training? How fast and how much rest between? How many minutes for the tempo runs? How many miles in the back-to-back workouts on the weekend? It is difficult to cram all that information into the tiny box representing a single day in a 12-week program, but we can fill in some of the numbers.

Most runners benefit from training that grows progressively harder as both their fitness improves and the date of their goal race approaches. I've examined a lot of training programs in books and magazines, programs designed by other writers and authors. Their programs all work that way. You begin in week 1 with a 90-minute long run and climax in week 11 with a two-hour long run, or whatever numbers in either miles or kilometers or minutes the coach has chosen. Here is a short summary of what to do each day of the week:

Monday

Mondays call for 3 miles (4.8 km) in week 1 and 3 miles in week 12. The distance remains the same over the length of the program, although I know some runners may want to add miles to increase their weekly and total mileage for the full program. Because this is a do-it-yourself program, you can make any changes you want.

Tuesday

For the first six weeks, alternate between hill training and interval training. Eight reps in week 1, then 9 × hill and 10 × hill in weeks 3 and 5. Use a similar progression on the interval training days: 10 × 400 meters at 5K pace, walking or jogging between. The last six weeks feature only interval training with the distances shifting upward to 800 meters and 1,600 meters.

Wednesday

This is a rest day, the same as on Mondays. I prescribe 3 miles (4.8 km) in the program I am designing; you get to choose your own distance. But don't overdo the number of miles run or the speed of those miles because this is supposed to be a recovery day between two days of speed work.

Thursday

The second speed workout of the week is a tempo run. It is not measured in distance but rather in time: 40 minutes in week 1; 60 minutes in week 11, the peak week before the taper in week 12, where the numbers all decrease.

Friday

This is a day of complete rest. No running. Can't handle a day off from running? I'm not going to trip you going out the door, but take it easy. You want to be rested for the weekend workouts. Every third week features a race (as shown in the following chart), meaning you want to do an easy run on Friday and rest on Saturday.

Saturday

This gets a little complicated. Moving from week 1 to week 2 to week 3, you first run at an easy pace, the next week run at your half marathon pace, and on the third week take a rest day before a Sunday race. Repeat that pattern three more times, and it brings you to week 12 and your half marathon.

Sunday

For advanced runners, I suggest thinking minutes, not miles. A 90-minute run in week 1 becomes a two-hour run in week 11. As with Saturday, the workout changes slightly in three-week batches. Moving from week 1 to week 2 to week 3, you first do a 3/1 run, easy the first three-fourths of the workout, then faster the final quarter; the next week you run easy for the full time, and the third week you run a race.

While I'm filling in those numbers, I also will make a few last-minute tweaks, adding 5K, 10K, and 15K races every third week in place of the Sunday long run. And before each of those races, I'll suggest a minitaper: rest or run on Friday, rest on Saturday, race on Sunday. (If the race is on Saturday, back up your taper one day.) In week 12, plan a final taper leading into the half marathon.

And finally, let's skip past advanced half marathon, which you can find in chapter 12. As long as we are playing with our computer toys, let's create a program one step higher and call it advanced 2 half marathon, with some slight tweaks upward, mostly designed to give you more total mileage each week and for the length of the program. Here is the final version of the do-it-yourself training program:

Week	Mon	Tue	Wed	Thu	Fri	Sat	Sun
1	3-mile run	8 × hill	3-mile run	40 min tempo	Rest	5-mile run	2:00 run (3/1)
2	3-mile run	10 × 400 m at 5K pace	3-mile run	45 min tempo	Rest	5-mile pace	2:00 run
3	3-mile run	9 × hill	3-mile run	30 min tempo	Rest or easy run	Rest	5K race
4	4-mile run	11 × 400 m at 5K pace	4-mile run	40 min tempo	Rest	6-mile run	2:20 run (3/1)
5	4-mile run	10 × hill	4-mile run	45 min tempo	Rest	6-mile pace	2:20 run
6	4-mile run	12 × 400 m at 5K pace	4-mile run	30 min tempo	Rest or easy run	Rest	10K race
7	5-mile run	6 × 800 m at 10K pace	5-mile run	45 min tempo	Rest	7-mile run	2:40 run (3/1)
8	5-mile run	5 × 1,600 m at race pace	5-mile run	50 min tempo	Rest	7-mile pace	2:40 run
9	5-mile run	7 × 800 m at 10K pace	5-mile run	30 min tempo	Rest or easy run	Rest	15K race
10	6-mile run	6 × 1,600 m at race pace	6-mile run	55 min tempo	Rest	8-mile run	3:00 run (3/1)
11	6-mile run	8 × 800 m at 5K pace	6-mile run	60 min tempo	Rest	8-mile pace	3:00 run
12	3-mile run	5 × 400 m at 5K pace	2 m run	30 min tempo	Rest	Rest	Half marathon

Note: To convert English distances to metric, use an online conversion website such as www.onlineconversion.com/length_common.

But here is a final tweak. The Bible tells us that God rested on the seventh day, and so we have that many days in each week. And to please the god of commerce (lower case), most of us work five days from Monday through Friday and take the weekend off, Saturday and Sunday. For that reason, most training programs, including all of mine, are designed on a seven-day matrix. But do we need to be trapped into those boxes?

David E. Martin, PhD, a Georgia State University exercise scientist and U.S. Olympic Committee consultant, didn't think so as he helped Keith Brantly prepare for the 1996 Olympic Games. Dave manipulated the traditional seven-days-a-week calendar and two-times-a-day regimen followed by most elite athletes to provide for additional hard workouts. Rather than having a hard day followed by an easy day followed by another hard and another easy day (four days, eight workouts), Dave asked Keith to do a hard run followed by two easy runs followed by the next hard run. Thus he ran a hard run in the morning, easy run in the evening and the next morning, and a hard run the next afternoon. This permitted Keith to fit more hard runs into a week of training: five hard workouts instead of the three or four following a program that offered a hard run only every other day.

Did it work? Keith had run 2:14:16, placing fourth in the 1992 U.S. Olympic Marathon Trials, missing the American team by only one place. Four years later, Keith improved his time by just under a minute, running 2:13:22, but most important, he finished in third place, qualifying him to compete in the 1996 Olympic Games in Atlanta, Georgia. Keith placed 22nd out of 111 marathoners, but perhaps most meaningful for those who respect how tough it is to reach the top of the pyramid, every time he walks into a group of runners, he is recognized as an Olympian.

But did Dave Martin's training pattern work? It's difficult to prove much from an experiment of one, but most important to me, the pair had broken the matrix or at least cracked it slightly.

Why a seven-day matrix? If you were a full-time runner, supported by a shoe company and other advertisers, living off your prize money, you would not need to be prisoner of a seven-day matrix into which a coach, like myself, could fit all the speed work into the middle of the week with the long runs on the weekend. Your needs differ from those tens of thousands of other runners finishing far behind you in half marathons. Consider instead a 10-day matrix, which would permit room for all the workouts needed to ensure marathon immortality.

Week	Mon	Tue	Wed	Thu	Fri	Sat	Sun
1	Short run	Hill training	Tempo run	Sorta-long run	Fartlek	Short run	Interval training
2	Rest	Pace run	Long run	–	–	–	–

That's the first 10 days. You could fill a full month, at least those featuring 30 days (30 days hath September) with three rounds of 10-day training. Either copy the pattern from the first 10 days and repeat it the next 10 days and the 10 days after, or get creative. Think outside the box. Move the workouts into different boxes, including some of the workouts (repeats, fartlek) that failed to make it into my other half marathon training programs.

Consider a second 10-day cycle, and there is no reason why it has to mirror the first 10-day cycle. In the first example, the emphasis was on speed with only one long run. For the second, let's shift the emphasis to endurance, including two long runs.

Week	Mon	Tue	Wed	Thu	Fri	Sat	Sun
3	–	–	–	Easy run	Sorta-long run	Tempo run	Pace run
4	Long run	Rest	Sorta-long run	Easy run	Pace run	Long run	–

Next is a third 10-day cycle, and in the spirit of the step-back weeks I use in many of my programs, make this an easy 10 days—or at least an *easier* 10 days than the other two. The first cycle emphasized speed. The second cycle emphasized endurance. This third cycle emphasizes what I might describe as dynamic recovery, not a complete break from training, but a blending of speed and endurance and rest.

Week	Mon	Tue	Wed	Thu	Fri	Sat	Sun
5	–	–	–	–	–	–	Easy run
6	Pace run	Rest	Tempo run	Sorta-long run	Easy run	Rest	Tempo run
7	Pace run	Sorta-long run	–	–	–	–	–

Finally, with the aplomb of a master cook, who knows what she is doing, who has at her elbow a favorite cookbook, here are the three 10-day cycles in a final 30-day cycle, a month's worth of training.

Week	Mon	Tue	Wed	Thu	Fri	Sat	Sun
1	Short run	Hill training	Tempo run	Sorta-long run	Fartlek	Short run	Interval training
2	Rest	Pace run	Long run	Easy run	Sorta-long run	Tempo run	Pace run
3	Long Run	Rest	Sorta-long run	Easy run	Pace run	Long run	Easy run
4	Pace run	Rest	Tempo run	Sorta-long run	Easy run	Rest	Tempo run
5	Pace run	Sorta-long run	–	–	–	–	–

Do I sense Russ Pate, my guardian angel, hovering over my shoulder shaking his head, maybe smiling? I suspect only a small percentage of runners could benefit from this radical a program, but why not write for such a small percentage? I only wish that such an approach, and such a training program, had been available when I wore a younger man's clothes. Would it have made me a better runner and allowed me to achieve attainable success? No proof that it would have or would not have. Let's not end with the suggestion that whether or not this do-it-yourself program could have made me faster. It certainly can make you faster, however. I offer it to you as an end point to the many training programs offered in *Hal Higdon's Half Marathon Training*.

Epilogue
Rocking the Half

On a sunny Saturday in summer, my wife, Rose, and I boarded a train at the Carroll Avenue station near our home in Michigan City, Indiana, and headed into Chicago. The South Shore Line is the only remaining electric interurban railroad in the United States and, as expressways become increasingly clogged with traffic, we find the train a pleasant alternative to car travel.

Others felt the same that weekend, the eight-car train being crammed with young people going into Chicago for either a Taylor Swift concert or a Blackhawks convention. Most were easily identifiable by clothing branded with their favorite singer or hockey player. Runners on the train seemed less identifiable. We had not yet claimed our Rock 'n' Roll Chicago Half Marathon shirts, which we would do at that race's expo at McCormick Place on the lakefront.

The ride into Chicago took just under two hours. Departing the train, we climbed a single flight of stairs that led upward into the mammoth hall and joined the stream of runners moving toward the expo. A buzz filled the air. No matter how many races I have run, no matter how many bibs I have attached to race singlets, no matter how many carbo dinners I have *glomped* down, I always find myself inspired by my fellow runners. Certainly, some in the passing stream spent the previous 12 weeks using one of my training programs. I felt invested in their commitment to run 13.1 miles the next day.

As I moved from the corridor into the main hall hosting the expo, it seemed fitting that, having begun this book describing the Indy Mini, I would end it with another major half marathon: Rock 'n' Roll Chicago. Big image events such as these are at the heart of the running movement today, particularly the explosion of interest in 13.1-mile races.

Entering the hall, I quickly picked up my bib and my shirt, then used my cell phone to call Dan Cruz, who supervises public relations for Competitor Group, the running behemoth that nurtures the Rock 'n' Roll races, both full and half marathons, 30 races worldwide with half a million participants. Dan told me he was off at the finish line in Grant Park supervising some last-minute details, but expected to return to the expo within the half hour.

That offered Rose and me an opportunity to wander the expo aisles, which is somewhat like being a kid invited to enter a toy shop. We encountered first a platform where three people at a time stomped rapidly on footplates to see who could push a toy runner up to the top of a mountain. Future Olympic event? What will they think up next to amuse fitness-minded people? Want a gait analysis to help in selecting your next shoe? Step onto our treadmill. Hats, visors, chocolate milk. Booths where other races hope to lure you to their starting lines. A sports car with bold letters on its hood: *Rock Your Run!* Sign up at a booth for free runner tracking that will allow you to follow your runner in the race by smart phone. Buy a watch that will map your run and count your calories. A long line had formed in front of one booth, but I didn't get close enough to see what was being given away. One needs to be careful about the free items you accept at an expo. Some years ago at the Chicago Marathon, I was signing and selling books next to a booth featuring free chili. I wanted to shout to those standing in line "Excuse me, people! Do you realize what you are about to eat?" I hoped that there were sufficient porta potties along the course.

There was no chili, thankfully, at Rock 'n' Roll, but one could find shoes, sport drinks, gels.

And bumper stickers for whatever distance you have run: 5K, 13.1, 26.2, 70.3, 100. My favorite: 0.0: I don't run. You could take a selfie in front of a wall proclaiming "Chicago. My Kind of Town." Another sign summarized what running races like Rock 'n' Roll is all about: "Run for the bling!"

Do we run for the bling? Is this why you bought my book? No one can deny that it's nice to cross the finish line and have a volunteer hang a ribboned medal around your neck, but we really run for our health, for fitness, for weight control, for guilt-free consumption of donuts, for PRs, for BQs (those Boston-qualifying times), for the feeling of the wind in our hair, for music in the case of the Rock 'n' Roll races. Does anybody get tired of having Bruce Springsteen belt out, "Born to Run"? We all come to the half marathon feast for different reasons, and this is how it should be. You don't need to explain your presence at the starting line. It's what you do; it's what we do.

By the time we had passed through every aisle and eyeballed every table, Dan Cruz returned from the finish line. We chatted briefly, but he was busy, and I was eager to get to our hotel to relax, so I thanked him for his hospitality and the media badge just handed to me.

Leaving the expo, we hailed a cab to head to our hotel, the Monaco, and immediately got caught in traffic because Taylor Swift or maybe the Blackhawks or maybe just because it was summer in the city. I instructed our cab driver to forget Lake Shore Drive and cut across 31st Street to Dr. Martin Luther King Jr. Drive, then across to Michigan Avenue. Having been born and raised in Chicago, I knew all the alternate routes to avoid traffic. Soon we reached the Monaco. After dinner, Rose and I strolled along the Riverwalk, a pathway beside the Chicago River, opened only recently, crammed with people enjoying a warm evening. A single jogger tried not too successfully to weave her way through the crowds. I suspected that she would not be running the half marathon the next morning.

Neither was I. Sorry to end this book by setting a terribly bad example, but writing about running sometimes absorbs so much psychic energy that my training suffers. While spending the winter in Florida, I had run the 5-mile (8 km) Winter Beach Run in February and the 15K (9.3 miles) Gate River Run in March, thus it should have been an easy jump to 13.1 miles, but I lacked the motivation to make that jump. At the Indy Mini, I ran the accompanying 5K, not the full 13.1. Although I had entered Rock 'n' Roll Chicago expecting to pay penance, sorry everybody. I decided later to enjoy the race as a spectator and reporter and save my next half marathon for later.

Thus, soon after sunrise on Sunday morning, while all the Taylor Swift and Blackhawks fans were sleeping, I positioned myself on the Randolph Street Bridge above Columbus Drive, about a half mile down course from the starting line, packed with nearly 15,000 runners. The bridge was crowded with other spectators, most of them holding cameras or smart phones to record the passage of a friend or family member.

Despite our distance from the starting line loudspeaker, I could hear the countdown: three, two, one, then a horn. Starting guns having become less fashionable since Boston 2013. The first wave of runners appeared, the fastest of the fast, fewer than a hundred in the first wave. They disappeared below me beneath the bridge turning right toward the lake. Then another wave of about two or three hundred runners, then another wave similar in size, then another and another and another until 2,000 cleared the line. I did not wait for the final waves, but took a shortcut to intercept the runners as they doubled back beside the Chicago River.

At the river, I descended a stairway to the level of the runners as they approached a river bridge where they turned right. I joined them, walking beside the flow snapping iPhone photos, which later I would upload to my Facebook page. Eventually, I exited the course at the point the field flowed beneath Michigan Avenue, Chicago's Magnificent Mile.

I followed Michigan back to the river and paused at the bridge next to the Wrigley Building. I could look upstream to see runners crossing the river heading north on Lake Shore Drive, then look downstream to runners heading south along State Street. Long before there was Rock 'n' Roll, either music or a race with music, engineers reversed the flow of the river into the lake, directing the water from the lake through the Chicago River to the Des Plaines River to the Illinois River and to the Mississippi River and ultimately to the Gulf of Mexico, connecting to all the waters of the world. The symbolism struck me: that in flowing through 13.1 miles of City of Chicago streets, these 15,000 runners were connecting also to the many more hundreds of thousands running half marathons all over the world.

It's Tribute Time

And so we come to the end of *Hal Higdon's Half Marathon Training*. It's tribute time. Let me pay tribute to all of those who made this book possible, beginning with Jason Muzinic, the acquisitions editor at Human Kinetics. Jason had worked with me in promoting *4:09:43*, my book on the Boston Marathon bombings. Soon after that book's publication, at the expo for the 2014 Boston Marathon, we discussed the possibility of my doing a training book for HK. It didn't take too much effort to convince Jason to focus our attention on the half marathon. I asked Jan Seeley, publisher of *Marathon & Beyond*, to act as my agent and work out the contractual details, easily done. Jason passed the project on to Liz Evans to handle the necessary editing.

Also involved in bringing this handbook to market at Human Kinetics are Nancy Rasmus and Maurey Williamson.

I have relied heavily on social media in gathering information. You already have encountered in these pages the names of my many research assistants. The stories and experiences of no less than 140 people are found here. These were people who responded to threads I started on my Facebook page asking about their training, their racing experiences, everything they learned running 13.1 miles. In this respect, the comments of a newbie runner who just started running a few weeks before can be just as valuable as the comments of coaches and scientists. As runners, we learn from each other. I have become a conduit that channels information from one runner to another rather than only a writer. Thanks to everybody so named and quoted who contributed to this book.

Finally, I'd like to thank my family, my wife, Rose, who has always supported me in a hobby, which eventually become a profession. She accepted me as a lifetime companion in an era where only the most talented runners would continue in their sport after graduating from high school or college, yet here was I going out for 20-mile runs along the Chicago lakefront while she took care of the three kids. At my first Boston Marathon in 1959, only 151 started. The half marathon? It barely existed as a race distance. No one then could have predicted that fields of 30,000 or more would be common at full-distance marathons around the world, and that a race half that classic distance would show that 13.1 was sometimes more than 26.2. Thanks to all of you who have made *Hal Higdon's Half Marathon Training* possible.

Bibliography

Anderson, Owen. 2013. *Running science*, Champaign, IL: Human Kinetics.

Benson, Roy T. 2003. *Coach Benson's "secret" workouts: Coachly wisdom for runners about effort-based training*, New York, Beaufort Books.

Benson, Roy, and Declan Connolly. 2011. *Heart rate training*, Champaign, Illinois: Human Kinetics.

Benyo, Richard, and Joe Henderson. 2002. *Running encyclopedia*, Champaign, IL: Human Kinetics.

Brown, Richard L. 2015. *Fitness running*, Champaign, IL: Human Kinetics.

Clark, Nancy. 2014. *Nancy Clark's sports nutrition guidebook*, Champaign, IL: Human Kinetics.

Daniels, Jack. 2014. *Daniels' running formula*, Champaign, IL: Human Kinetics.

Davis, John. 2013. *Modern training and physiology for middle and long-distance runners*, Eden Prairie, MN: Running Writings.

Fenton, Mark. 2008. *The complete guide to walking for health, weight loss and fitness*, Guilford, CT: Lyons Press.

Higdon, Hal. 1997a, *Hal Higdon's Beginning Runner's Guide*, Long Beach, IN, Roadrunner Press.

Higdon, Hal. 1997b. *Hal Higdon's how to train: The best programs, workouts, and schedules for runners of all ages*, Emmaus, PA: Rodale Press.

Humphrey, Luke, Keith Hanson, and Kevin Hanson. 2014. *Hansons half-marathon method: Run your best half-marathon the Hansons way*, Boulder, CO: VeloPress.

Martin, David E., and Peter N. Coe. 1991. *Training distance runners*, Champaign, IL: Leisure Press.

McGregor, Stephen, and Matt Fitzgerald. 2010. *The runner's edge*, Champaign, IL: Human Kinetics.

Milroy, Andy. 2012. "The origins of the marathon," originally published in *The Analytical Distance Runner*, edited by Ken Young.

Noakes, Timothy. 2001. *Lore of running*, Champaign, IL: Human Kinetics.

Pfitzinger, Pete, and Scott Douglas. 2009. *Advanced marathoning*, Champaign, IL: Human Kinetics.

Pfitzinger, Pete, and Philip Latter. 2015. *Faster road racing: 5K to half marathon*, Champaign, IL: Human Kinetics.

Utzschneider, Cathy. 2014. *Mastering running*, Champaign, IL: Human Kinetics.

Utzschneider, Cathy. 2014. *Mastering the half marathon eBook*, Champaign, IL: Human Kinetics.

Van Allen, Jennifer, Bart Yasso, Amby Burfoot, and Pamela Nisevich Bede. 2012. *The Runner's World big book of marathon and half marathon training: Winning strategies, inspiring stories, and the ultimate training tools*, Emmaus, PA: Rodale Press.

About the Author

Hal Higdon has contributed to *Runner's World* for longer than any other writer. An article by Hal appeared in that publication's second issue in 1966. Author of more than 36 books, including the best-selling *Marathon: The Ultimate Training Guide* (Rodale, 2011), *4:09:43: Boston 2013 Through the Eyes of the Runners* (Human Kinetics, 2014), and *RunFast* (Rodale, 2000). Higdon has also written books on many subjects and for various age groups. His children's book *The Horse That Played Center Field* was made into an animated feature by ABC TV.

He ran eight times in the Olympic Trials and won four World Masters Championships. One of the founders of the Road Runners Club of America, Higdon was a finalist in NASA's Journalist-in-Space program to ride the space shuttle. He has served as training consultant for the Chicago Marathon and Chicago Area Runners Association and also answers questions on Facebook, offering interactive training programs through TrainingPeaks and apps through Bluefin. At the annual meeting of the American Society of Journalists and Authors in 2003, Higdon received the Career Achievement Award, the highest honor given to writer members.

Higdon became acquainted with the Boston Marathon as a member of the U.S. Army stationed in Stuttgart, Germany, training with Dean Thackwray, who would make the U.S. Olympic team in 1956. Higdon knew then that he eventually needed to shift his focus from his usual track events (including the 3,000-meter steeplechase) to the marathon. He first ran Boston in 1959, then again in 1960, failing to finish both years. "My mistake," Higdon realized later, "was trying to win the race, not finish the race."

It took five years for Higdon to figure out the training necessary for success as an elite marathoner, becoming the first American finisher (fifth overall) in 1964. The previous year, he wrote an article for *Sports Illustrated* about Boston titled "On the Run From Dogs and People" (later a book by the same title) that contributed to the explosion of interest in running in the 1970s that continues to this day.

Higdon also wrote a coffee table book titled *Boston: A Century of Running*, published before the 100th running of the Boston Marathon in 1996. An expanded version of a chapter in that book featuring the 1982 battle between Alberto Salazar and Dick Beardsley, titled *The Duel*, continues as a best-seller among running books.

Higdon has run 111 marathons, 18 of them at Boston. He considers himself more than a running specialist, having spent most of his career as a full-time journalist writing about a variety of subjects, including business, history, and science, for publications such as *Reader's Digest*, *Good Housekeeping*, *National Geographic*, and *Playboy*. Among his more than three dozen published books are two involving major crimes: *The Union vs. Dr. Mudd* (about the Lincoln assassination) and *The Crime of the Century* (about the Leopold and Loeb case, featuring attorney Clarence Darrow). The 2014 publication of *4:09:43: Boston 2013 Through the Eyes of the Runners* resonated with the worldwide community of runners deeply affected by the bombings at the 2013 Boston Marathon.

Higdon continues to run and bike with his wife, Rose, from their winter and summer homes in Florida and Indiana. They have three children and nine grandchildren.